TREASURES OF
ANCIENT
GREECE

TREASURES OF
ANCIENT
GREECE

JOHN S BOWMAN

GALLERY BOOKS
An imprint of W.H. Smith Publishers Inc.
112 Madison Avenue
New York, New York 10016

A Bison Book

Published by Gallery Books
A Division of W H Smith Publishers Inc.
112 Madison Avenue
New York, New York 10016

Produced by
Bison Books Corp.
17 Sherwood Place
Greenwich, CT 06830

ISBN 0-8317-8813-5

Printed in Hong Kong

1 2 3 4 5 6 7 8 9 10

Oversize
DF
77
.B67
1986

Page 1: The Temple of Apollo, Corinth.
Pages 2–3: The Hephaistion stands high above the Agora,
Athens.
Pages 4–5: The Avenue of the Lions at Delos.

Contents

1. Dawn in the Aegean

The cradle of civilization . . . The golden age . . . The treasures of Greece. . .' How easily these phrases roll off the tongue, and how glibly they are absorbed into the consciousness. For everyone 'knows' what is being referred to: Athens, and in particular, classical Athens of the fifth century BC – that is, about 500 to 400 BC, a period extended at most to the surrounding sites of Attica and from 550 to 350 BC. But there it is: the treasure-chest of our civilization, Greece.

Or so it once was. Today, our view of ancient Greece has greatly changed – indeed, it has not been so confined for some 50 to 100 years, at least for those who have kept abreast of modern scholarship in such fields as archaeology and art history. Today our view of Greece's history is far more multilayered, complex, sophisticated. The notion that classical Athens miraculously emerged full-grown – like Athena from the brow of Zeus in the myth – has given way to quite a different version in which Greek history and culture extends over a much greater time period. It is no longer confined to the city-state of Athens or sur-rounding Attica, nor even to the adjacent Greek mainland.

If it is now accepted that Greece extends much farther in space and time, the concept of its 'treasures' has equally expanded beyond the image of white marble columns, statues in repose and 'Grecian urns.' Our view of Greek art and architecture now incorporates a much more heterogeneous, dynamic and richer achievement. It may be less 'classical' and less idealized, but it is certainly more stimulating and far truer to the realities of ancient Greece.

Consider the matter of just who the ancient Greeks were. If the word were to be restricted to those people who spoke the language we today recognize as Greek, then Greek art and architecture may not be thought

Above: An early Neolithic cult figure of a goddess from Knossos dates back to 4000 BC.
Left: A Neolithic pottery *kemos* for ritual incense burning is decorated with paint and incising.
Right: The formal lines of the Cycladic marble idols were created with simple copper tools and a local abrasive, carborundum. These abstract figures were sculpted *c* 2500 BC.

Preceding pages: The Cyclopean stone blocks of the Queen's staircase at the Palace of Knossos are supported by richly painted columns.

of as beginning until 2000 BC at the earliest. But if this word is accepted as applying to those various peoples who have inhabited the territory – mainland and islands – that we today know as the nation-state of Greece, then Greece can lay claim to a still richer storehouse of treasures. The tendency now is to employ 'Greek' in this latter sense, if for no other reason than that it is recognized that there was an unending chain of interactions and influences among the various peoples who inhabited Greek territory over the millennia.

It is known, for instance, that the first human beings to live in Greece settled there at least as far back as 75,000 years ago; there were few of them, they lived in isolated groups – evidently in a few caves – and their culture was of the basic Paleolithic ('Old Stone Age') variety; in any case, they seem to have left no legacy, either in terms of population or culture, to the people who appear in the Neolithic ('New Stone Age') period. These Neolithic Greeks appeared sometime around 7000 BC, but who they were, racially or physically, is not known for sure; they spoke some non-Greek language that was probably related to languages spoken by people in Asia Minor and the Near East – presumably their homeland, although they may also have moved down from Balkan Europe after some centuries there.

These first Neolithic Greeks were already farmers, herders and fishermen before moving into Greece, and either brought the actual objects of Neolithic culture – seeds, animals, tools they had developed elsewhere – or the knowledge and techniques to exploit their new environment as they had their homeland. During the next few thousands of years bands of migrants, possibly whole tribes and maybe some individual stragglers, continued to move into the Greek mainland and islands, settling first in Macedonia, the northern stretch of Greece, and then in Thessaly, the north-central region of the mainland. Village settlements began to develop – Nea Nikomedia in Macedonia by about 6500 BC, Sesklo and Dimini in Thessaly in ensuing millennia. By 3000 BC there were Neolithic settlements throughout much of Greece, from Macedonia to Crete and from Athens to Samos.

Meanwhile, Neolithic people in Asia Minor and the Near East had developed a truly revolutionary invention: pottery. They seem to have made the first pottery by about 6500 BC, and both their artefacts and techniques spread quickly across the Aegean and into Greece, either with migrants or traders. The first pottery was simple in form and with a plain, dark burnished surface; any color variations resulted from the firing process. But by about 6000 BC, the people of Asia Minor and the Near East were developing painted pottery, a style the Greeks were also quick to adopt. Painted pottery began with simple, geometric designs of red on a light surface, but ceramics soon blossomed into a garden of decorative motifs, shapes and functions. At Nea Nikomedia, people were soon shaping pots with human faces on the surface by pinching a 'nose' and adding ovals of clay for 'eyes,' suggesting these early Greeks may well have had a sense of humor.

Another element of Neolithic culture that spread throughout the Aegean area and Greece was the small, sculptured figurine, usually female. In fact, such figurines go far back into Paleolithic times in Europe, where from 25,000 BC onwards people made them out of stone, ivory or clay. Over thousands of years these figurines inevitably took on many forms, from the very crude through the quite naturalistic to the highly stylized. The makers seldom devoted much attention to the head or features but emphasized the female sexual characteristics – breasts, genitalia and buttocks. (The fat buttocks, in fact, have lent their Greek epithet, *steatopygous*, to certain of these figurines.) Today we can only speculate about the significance of these figurines for the Neolithic people, but they most likely had something to do with the religious beliefs of the time. Certainly in this early Greek world the various aspects of the female – as procreator and nurturer – seem to have merged into the image of the Great Mother, or Nature Goddess, who was to permeate Mediterranean religious life for many centuries.

By about 5000 BC, a quite different new principle had also appeared on the Greek scene: metallurgy. People in the highlands of Asia Minor and Iran or in the Danube valley seem to have been the first to work with metal – this was about 6500 BC and the metal was copper. The use of metals spread slowly and for many centuries only the élite employed metal for exceptional or luxury objects – a ceremonial blade, some special ornament – and most people continued with the Neolithic culture. This transitional period is now known as the Chalcolithic ('Copper-stone') Age in recognition of this long lag.

So, too, when bronze – an alloy of copper and tin – was introduced sometime around 3000 BC, people did not convert *en masse* to making objects out of the new metal. But just as agriculture came to trigger off a whole series of developments that made up the Neolithic Revolution, so bronze began to signal a series of changes: tin and copper, for instance, usually had to be mined or extracted in separate places, often far removed, then shipped to a third place where they could be combined by special processing. This meant more than transportation and technical problems; it became a matter of communication, both in the literal sense of languages and in the broader sense of cultural contacts. This in turn led to social ferment and the release of new energies, often involving the movements of peoples.

Among those to profit from this Bronze Age traffic among the many communities in the Greek world were the inhabitants of the Cyclades, a group of numerous islands in the southern part of the Aegean, of which Melos, Syros, Keos, Thera (Santorini), Naxos, Delos and Mykonos are probably the most renowned, giving their name to the distinctive Bronze Age culture that developed on these islands in the years following 3000 BC. The Cycladic islanders had long participated in the network of cultural influences and economic interactions that formed the greater Greek world. Their own resources were, however, limited mainly to minerals: the obsidian of Melos had been sought out since about 7500 BC for making sharp tools, but there was also marble and other valued stone on these islands. In the Bronze Age, the Cycladic islanders moved beyond exporting raw materials and became enterprising producers of fine ceramic and stone vases. And Cycladic islanders appear to have shown great concern for their dead, for they buried with them marble statues – some so small they fit into the palm of one's hand, some fully lifesize. Most of them are female figurines, suggestive of the age-old belief in the Nature Goddess who promoted fertility; but beyond that, the carving of these figures was so consciously controlled and elegant that they rank among the most sophisticated works of art of any people before the classic Greeks.

As the Cycladic islanders were developing, people elsewhere in Greece were also moving in their own ways. Most of the mainland Greeks were descendants of the Neolithic peoples, on many of whose earliest sites they continued to rebuild and live. There may have been some new migrants and some increased contacts with Europeans to the north and others; so although these mainland inhabitants were essentially part of the broader Aegean Bronze Age, their particular variety of culture is known as Helladic. Yet even though such Helladic sites as Lerna were flourishing between about 2500–2200 BC, no speakers of Greek or its parent language are known to have appeared in the Greek mainland or islands.

Above: Painted votive figures made of pottery were found throughout the Minoan Empire.
Right: A marble figure of a seated harpist from the Cyclades shows the early development of sculpture in the round.

And in one part of the Greek world, still another and very special culture was developing by this time – again by a non-Greek-speaking people. This was on Crete, which had been originally settled by Neolithic people starting about 6500 BC; evidently these first Cretans came from the Near East or Asia Minor. For hundreds and then thousands of years, Cretans shared the way of life of most Neolithic peoples, not only throughout Greece but throughout the populated world. Yet some Cretans made contacts with the world outside, and their early pottery shows the influence of Egypt and other cultures to the east. But it was not until sometime after 3000 BC that something happened to lift Crete out of the Neolithic rut. Possibly it was only that the indigenous Cretans were sharing in the 'leap forward' of the Bronze Age. More likely a new group of migrants arrived, although they probably came from the same place or places as the original Cretans – Asia Minor, the shores of the Levant. Probably, too, they did not differ that much in appearance or language from those people already on Crete. And whether or not these newcomers imposed themselves on the natives by force, they began to exert a strong influence on Cretan life, at least by 2500 BC. These new Cretans, for instance, seem to have been more energetic, more outgoing, more open to change, and probably led the way by introducing more advanced artefacts and techniques, notably metallurgy and bronze.

Naturally, not everyone all over Crete began to use metals, any more than all Bronze Age communities began to advance simultaneously and at the same pace. There would always be differences between settlements and regions throughout Greece. But here and there throughout eastern and central Crete – particularly at sites like Knossos, Phaestos, Mallia and on the south-central plain, the Messara – people began to move ahead in the centuries following 2500 BC. Drawing upon both native and imported materials and talents, techniques and concepts, Cretans began to shape a Bronze Age culture that was distinctive enough to become known (even to the classic Greeks) as 'Minoan.' (This name was derived from Minos, the legendary king, but seems to refer to a title

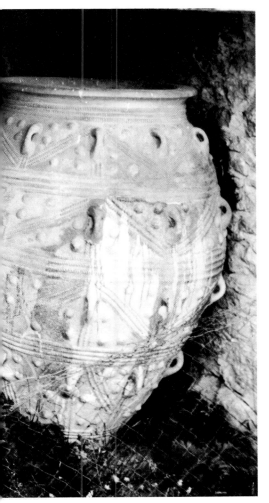

assumed by a whole dynasty of kings.)

The Minoans of the years between 2500–2000 BC, for instance, were already making pottery in varied forms, styles and designs. They fashioned hard stones into vases, adapting the veined or mottled textures of the stone to the shape and function of the vessels or incising or inlaying the surface of the vases. They produced beautiful gold ornaments, eventually making use of such sophisticated techniques as filigree and granulation. The Minoans may have learned some of these techniques from individual migrants or from their contacts abroad, in particular, with their stone vases they seem to have been imitating the Egyptians. But in most of their work, from these earliest centuries to their declining years, the Minoans infused traditional forms with their own observations of plants and animals to create a recognizable and consistent Minoan culture – one that seems consistent with what we today regard as the Greek tradition.

These early Minoans were already trading and colonizing around the greater Aegean world – certain Cycladic islands seem to have become virtually Minoan dependencies – but despite their economic initiatives, the Minoans did not develop any particular political structures to govern their own island up to about 2000 BC. Shortly thereafter Knossos, Phaestos and Mallia, long the sites of major settlements, emerged as power bases of Crete's growing population, increasing urbanization and expanding economy. The chieftains of these centers probably respected each other's domains – Mallia covering the east, Phaestos the south and Knossos the north-central region – but the leader of Knossos seems to have emerged as 'first among equals.'

Knossos, Phaestos and Mallia never seem to have drawn upon military force; their strength was sustained, rather, by some combination of land and its produce along with the products of trade and handicrafts. Whatever the source of their wealth, these centers began to

erect far more ambitious structures than Cretans had seen before on their island – multistoried buildings around courtyards with corridors and stairways, living quarters, workshops and ceremonial chambers. With spring water brought in through terracotta pipes (at Knossos, from some 10 miles away) and rainwater collected in cisterns, they were truly worthy of being called palaces. And when about 1700 BC some massive earthquake or series of earthquakes almost totally destroyed these great palaces, the Minoans quickly recovered and set about building still grander palaces on these very sites.

The palaces inevitably had first call on the finest talents and products of Crete, and there were workshops where pottery, stonemasons and jewellers practiced their skills. And as the centers of economic and political life, the palaces drew upon tribute and taxes; there were storerooms for the great urns of oil, wine and grain, while various bureaucrats and clerks recorded and regulated the flow of produce and products with a linear script on clay tablets.

Fine workmanship, in small details as well as of major architectural forms, distinguished the palaces of the Minoans. Most stunning of all were the many walls that the Minoans painted with frescoes. Some of the paintings were purely decorative motifs but many represented the

Above: Storage vases from Knossos with decoration of stylized double-axe or *labrys*.
Above right: Detail of vase from Knossos shows the beginnings of naturalism in design. This trend is thought to be an Egyptian influence.
Top far left: A large *krater* from about *c* 1750 BC, for mixing wine, was found in a wall cupboard at the Palace of Phaistos.
Top left: Small pottery cup with painted scroll decoration, found at Knossos.
Left: Painted Minoan storage vases with stylized decorations of scrolls and grain.

island's plants and animals or the ceremonies and activities of the Minoans themselves. The bright colors and imaginative forms of these frescoes must have added greatly to the sense of vitality around the palaces.

With the increased complexity of social, economic and political structures, religion also became more elaborate; a priestly hierarchy, rituals, cults and beliefs now developed around the traditional core of religion that had permeated the Aegean world through the Neolithic and still older ages. The Minoans seem to have centered their worship on the Great Mother and her fertility cults, and they continued to make the female figurines but now in more elaborate variations. They also intensified and diversified the primitive belief in natural forces into a more sophisticated pantheism, with the god-spirit manifest in many forms of nature: birds, trees, earthquakes, thunder and snakes, for instance, all had their sacred aspects. And drawing upon still other currents within the religious life of the ancient world, the Minoans adopted such symbols as the horns of consecration and the double axe; both of these may well have been involved in some ritual sacrifice of the bull, for it was this animal that the Minoans seem to have identified as their sacred and totemic spirit. The supreme event of their ceremonial life seems to have been the bull-leaping, held in special arenas where highly trained young men and women approached the onrushing bull, grasped its horns, arched themselves over the bull's back and landed on their feet behind it. And, however bizarre it must seem, the religious spirit must have pervaded the occasion as it did everything else in Minoan life.

During the centuries between, say, 2000–1500 BC, many Minoans were freeing themselves from the natural cycles of the soil and sea that governed the mass of people's lives. They were taking up crafts in the palace centers, some of which were centuries old, such as making pottery or stone vases, engraving seal-stones or molding clay figurines for votive offerings. But many men were taking up new jobs. Some had to make the many bronze objects – weapons such as large swords or delicate daggers, tools, containers, ceremonial axes. And in addition to requiring many skilled laborers and artisans, Minoan society offered careers in government, public works, farm estates and commerce. Above all, Minoan society prospered through the efforts of those engaged in maritime trade – sailors and dockworkers, importers and exporters, merchants and bureaucrats.

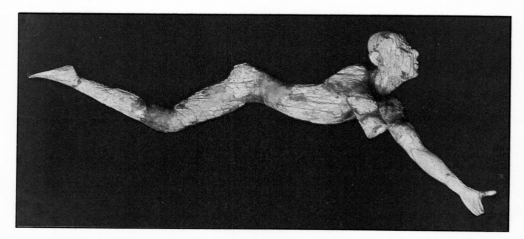

Left: An ivory figurine of an acrobat from Knossos. This could be part of a sculpture of the ritual of bull-leaping.
Below left: A *rhyton* or drinking cup of black steatite with scenes of wrestling, boxing and the capture of wild bulls.
Right: Stylized bulls' horns, one of the sacred symbols of the Minoan cult, were found on the roof lines of Cretan palaces.
Below: The so-called 'Harvesters Vase' from Hagia Triada, with its festive procession of countrymen, dates back to 1600 BC.

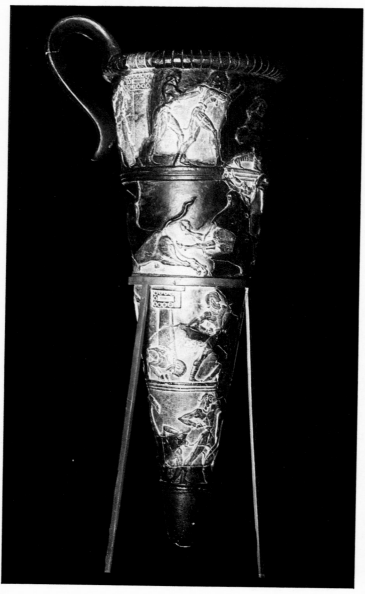

Above: Late Minoan pottery, *c* 1300–1250 BC, used natural decoration such as the octopus and waterfowl, similar to that used on Mycenaean ware.

Top left: A painted *larnax* or sarcophagus from Knossos. The rings on the side are thought to be for carrying poles.

Below far left: A pottery jug, decorated with a pattern of reeds, *c* 1600 BC.

Below left: Libation jug decorated with raised and stylized aquatic forms. Such jugs were used for religious offerings.

It was this commercial and maritime enterprise that later Greeks would describe as a *thalassocracy*, a 'sea empire' headed by Minos, king of Knossos. Perhaps the ruler of Knossos exacted a share of much that was exchanged by Minoan traders; undoubtedly, too, Minoan merchant ships were ready to engage in a little piracy, an accepted practice in those days. But although the sheer size and energy of the Minoan fleet made it a power to be reckoned with, the Minoans hardly maintained an empire in the modern sense of a centrally controlled power that imposes itself on foreigners with an explicit strategy and organized tactics.

But even a commercial empire is only as strong as its home base, and the Minoans controlled their domestic economy through their palace centers by keeping records and accounts. Simple pictographic scripts had been used on Crete since about 2000 BC, but from about 1700 BC some Minoan scribes began to set down business transactions and keep accounts in another script, now known as Linear A, recording an as yet unknown language but almost certainly neither Greek nor a direct relative. Then, certainly by 1480 BC, a new script now known as Linear B came into use, not only at Knossos but at centers on the Greek mainland. Linear B recorded mainly economic operations – inventories of herds, vases or furnishings, payments for commodities of labor or lists of ceremonial offerings. But modern man has been able to fill in certain gaps in Minoan writing, and it is now known that Linear B was an adaptation of the Linear A script accommodating a new language in use on Crete: Linear B was, in fact, an early form of Greek.

For the first time, then, evidence of the presence of Greeks – in the linguistic sense – appears. This might mean nothing more than that the Cretan scribes were speakers of Greek from the mainland and that, since most people had nothing to do with writing, they chose to use their own language. It is far more likely, however, that Greek-speaking people had gained control of Minoan Crete – or at least of Knossos – by about 1480 BC. How these people gained control on Crete is not known, but the distribution of Linear B tablets, as well as of Minoan artefacts, on the Greek mainland about this time indicates that the Greek-

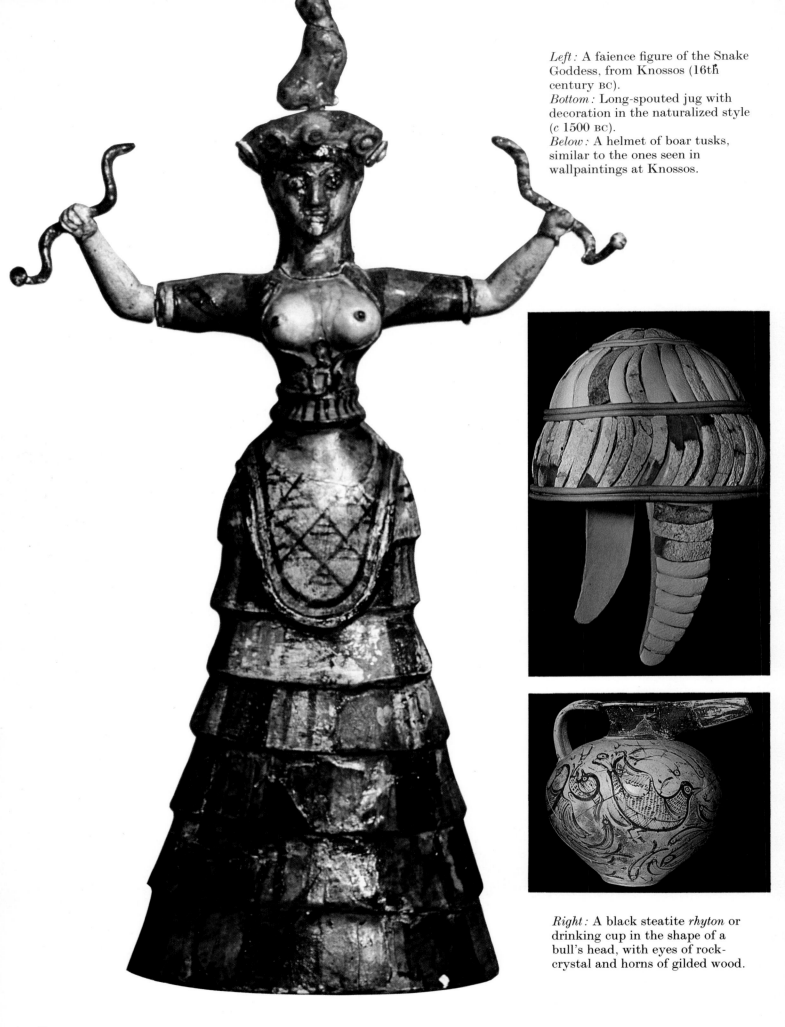

Left : A faience figure of the Snake Goddess, from Knossos (16th century BC).
Bottom : Long-spouted jug with decoration in the naturalized style (*c* 1500 BC).
Below : A helmet of boar tusks, similar to the ones seen in wallpaintings at Knossos.

Right : A black steatite *rhyton* or drinking cup in the shape of a bull's head, with eyes of rock-crystal and horns of gilded wood.

speaking people we know today as Mycenaeans (or Achaeans) were replacing the Minoans as the main power in this part of the Mediterranean.

It is not known exactly when these first Greek-speaking people appeared in the land we call Greece, but they seem to have moved in some time shortly after 2000 BC. Exactly where they came from is not known, but it was presumably somewhere to the northeast of Greece; they may well have been related to the Hittites of Anatolia or western Asia Minor, who also spoke an Indo-European language. But wherever they came from, these Achaean Greeks were neither roving coastal mariners nor settled farming folk. They were, rather, a seminomadic people who moved with their herds and the season – and if all of them weren't necessarily warlike, there were warriors among them, well armed and ready to take whatever they needed. Their culture, however, was in many ways more backward than that of the Helladic people; the so-called Minyans who appeared in Greece after 1900 BC seem to have had a rather limited repertoire of pottery.

The Achaeans may have initially caused a regression in mainland culture, but they by no means wiped out the indigenous Helladic peoples. They interacted with the more stable natives, even taking over many of the age-old mainland settlements. Before the Achaeans could begin to move ahead, however, they had much to learn, and they seem to have learned from the best teachers in the eastern Mediterranean at this time, the Minoans. During the centuries following 2000 BC, Crete – with its ships coming and going, its importing and exporting, its establishing of trading posts and colonies – acted as a magnet and set up a 'force-field' that energized surrounding lands and peoples. The Greek mainlanders were among those most receptive to such contacts, as when Minoan potters, metalworkers, jewellers and other artisans came over to the mainland to fashion their wares and impart their techniques.

All these sources – the indigenous Helladic, the imported Minoan and the emergent Achaeans – mingled to form what became the mainstream of early Greek culture. By 1600 BC, a strong, confident people was ready to assert itself on the Greek mainland; all that remained was for some individuals or place to provide the impetus. That seems to have come from Mycenae, an Achaean stronghold in the Peloponnesos. Mycenae had been inhabited since early Helladic times, but by 1600 BC it emerged as a center, if not the prime leader, of the Achaeans. Famed in ancient myth and legend, Mycenae was to give its name to the whole cultural phase of the early Greek people.

In the decades following 1600 BC, a succession of chieftain kings ruled at Mycenae. Exactly what they commanded in life is not known, but in their deaths they could call on tremendous resources. They buried their most honored dead, the royal élite – sometimes with their wives and children – in two cemeteries about 180 yards apart, each eventually surrounded by circular walls. On various bodies, they placed golden crowns and diadems, gold signet rings, belts of solid gold, silver jewelry; on the garments they attached large dress pins with crystal beads and sewed plaques in the shapes of butterflies or octopuses; alongside the bodies they placed vases of gold, silver, alabaster and finely painted clay; with the men they buried virtual armories – knives, daggers and swords, some of them gold-mounted and some with bronze blades inlaid with gold and silver. And on the faces of the most prominent chieftains they laid masks hammered out of sheet gold.

The rich and powerful élite of Mycenae used these shaft graves for at least a century after 1600 BC. About 150 years later, they began to build a different type: the *tholos* tomb, a large, circular vaulted chamber

Above: The entrance to a *tholos* tomb at Mycenae, constructed with gigantic stones. These walls were said to have been built by the Cyclops.
Top right: The Acropolis at Mycenae was built to take advantage of the terrain, high above the Argolid Plain.
Right: The Lion Gate at the entrance to the grave circle at Mycenae.

of stone often partly underground and approached by a passageway, or *dromos*, lined with stones. Within these great tombs, they dug pits into which they lowered the bodies; over the graves they made pyres in which they burned offerings on behalf of the dead. The Mycenaeans — and this term includes the residents of the many contemporary Greek settlements who were also constructing *tholos* tombs — buried riches in the pits equal in splendor to those in the shaft graves: gold jewelry, vases embossed in gold and silver, figurines in bronze and ivory and furniture adorned with ivory. But it was the *tholos* tombs themselves that expressed how far the Mycenaeans had advanced: the people responsible for such structures had not only mastered the engineering problems of weight and stress but also displayed a sense of architecture that went far beyond the piles of stones characteristic of most constructions of the era.

Above: The royal grave circles at Mycenae, separate from remaining tombs, were described by Pausanias in the second century AD as the tombs of Agamemnon and Clytemnestra.

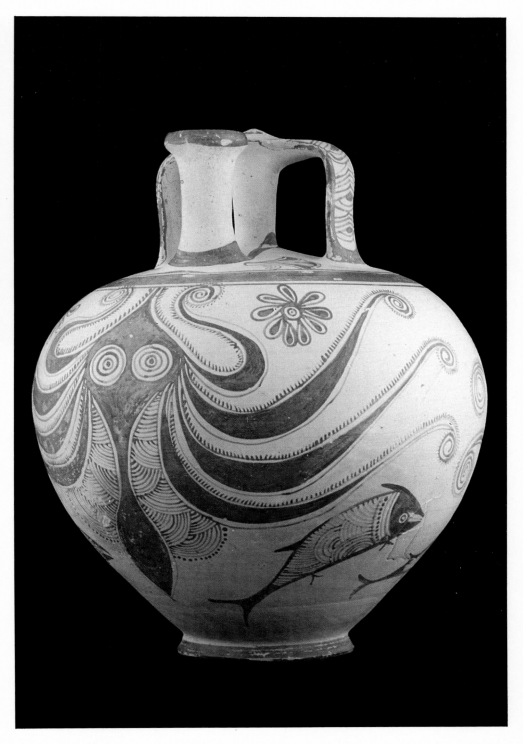

Above: 'The Mask of Agamemnon,' discovered by Heinrich Schliemann during excavations at Mycenae in the nineteenth century, is a magnificent example of beaten gold.
Right: Terracotta octopus jar (*c* 1200 BC). Despite the aquatic decoration, similar to the Minoan, this piece is Mycenaean.

Although there was a definite indigenous feel to the workmanship of the Mycenaeans, these graves also speak of the many foreign roots and links of their culture. Various peoples in Anatolia and the Near East, for instance, had been making shaft graves, while the Minoans had earlier built *tholos* tombs. And Egypt's influence on all its contemporaries should never be underestimated. But of all the different cultures that contributed to the Mycenaeans, the Minoans appear to have been the principal influence. This was to be expected because, at least until about 1500 BC, the Minoans remained the major economic-cultural force in the Aegean-Greek world. Minoan style and workmanship set the standards of the day in pottery, gold and silver objects, weapons, sealstones and many other crafts; wealthy Mycenaeans treasured their Minoan wares so highly that they chose to have them at their side for the afterlife.

Below: The remains of the *megaron* or great banqueting hall of the Palace at Tiryns, another Bronze Age kingdom.
Left: Cyclopean walls at the upper gateway of the citadel at Tiryns.

But at some point, as has been noted, the balance tilted in the other direction when the Mycenaeans began to usurp the Minoans' power and position in the Greek-Aegean world. Although it is not known for certain how this came about, it is fair to say that by about 1500 BC the Mycenaeans were coming into their own as an eastern Mediterranean economic power and a distinct Bronze Age Greek people. We know that Mycenaeans occupied Knossos and at least a few other Minoan centers on Crete about this time, but during their peak years – from about 1450 to 1250 BC – the Mycenaeans' culture centered on their own mainland palace-citadels, something between manor-estates and city-states. Mycenae itself was the most prominent by every measure, and was especially striking because of its location – on a high hill overlooking the great plain and gulf of Argos.

In quantitative terms – size of palace walls, number of communities, total population – the Mycenaeans probably attained their peak around 1300 BC; but in an ultimately more crucial qualitative sense they were also beginning to decline at about this time. Where they had once exhibited a certain cosmopolitan skill in such things as fresco painting, vase decoration or gem engraving, they now began to betray a provincialism in their arts and crafts. The Egyptians stopped importing Mycenaean pottery in such quantities as before; at Mycenae itself there was an end to the building of *tholos* tombs. For all their achievements, the Mycenaeans had many limitations: they were earthbound rather than aspiring, imitative rather than innovative. Although they can take credit for the strengths of an austere, hardy, pragmatic folk, they must also take responsibility for their lack of the liberating spirit of creativity.

Then, too, there was always an aggressive, bellicose streak in the Achaean character and as early as 1400 BC it was beginning to come to the fore. Weapons and walls had always been present in their culture; now armaments and fortifications became prominent. They did not set out on any campaign of conquest; indeed, much of the fighting was probably the Achaeans brawling among themselves – resentful, perhaps, that one palace-citadel or another was becoming too expansive. In any case, between about 1400 and 1250 BC, while the Mycenaeans were renovating and enlarging many of their palace-citadels, they were also making them more fortress-like. (It was the structures of this period at Mycenae, Pylos, Tiryns and elsewhere that were to be unearthed in a later age.) These great stone structures were so awesome that when the classic Greeks came upon their remains they attributed them to the Cyclopes, mythical giants.

Meanwhile, an event took place on a distant coast of the Aegean that involved the Mycenaeans. Over at Troy, where there had been continuous rebuilding of cities on the same old site, Troy VII had risen after some natural disaster destroyed Troy VI about 1300 BC. Then, about 1260 BC, this Troy VII seems to have been placed under siege; in any case, it was attacked, pillaged and burned. If ever there had

Above: Fresco fragments of a Mycenaean woman, perhaps during a harvest festival. Such frescoes were found on house and palace walls.
Right: Within the thickness of the Cyclopean walls at Tiryns are galleries with corbelled vaults.

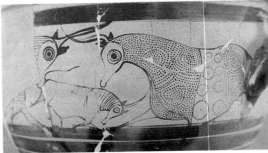

Above: The ritual *labrys* or double-axe was also used as a decorative motif on jugs and other pottery.
Left: Despite landslides and earthquakes, the strength of the walls of Tiryns is still evident, as is the manner of construction.
Top: Mycenaean pottery was frequently decorated with hunting scenes or paintings of domestic animals.

been a real Trojan War as described in the *Iliad* – the epic first written down some 500 years later – this city was probably the Troy that Agamemnon and his compatriots destroyed. For whatever reason – to gain or protect a trade route, to avenge some insult to an individual or a people – a coalition of Mycenaean city-states seem to have attacked this Troy. If so, they were probably fighting distant cousins, for the Trojans and the Achaeans of this time were probably descendants of the same people. Ironically, too, this obscure war, for which the Mycenaeans were to gain immortality, was to prove the swansong of their own culture.

For it was in the decades after 1260 BC that the major Mycenaean palace-citadels on the mainland were burned to the ground. A large part of the total community of Mycenae was destroyed and nearby Tiryns was overwhelmed and burned, while various other Mycenaean-Achaean centers were also destroyed. Even on Crete, the once ambitious Minoan-Mycenaean centers were allowed to fall into disrepair, and although the decline may have begun with a simple loss of energy it seems to have ended with the takeover by invaders.

Who were these destroyers of the Mycenaean mainland centers and the invaders of Crete? It cannot be established for sure, but it appears

Above: The familiar octopus remained a popular decoration on pottery after the fall of the Minoan Empire. The conquering Mycenaeans used it on wine and water containers.

Right: The Mycenaean stronghold of Orchomenos in Boetia was, like Mycenae, 'rich in gold.' The so-called 'Treasury of Minyas,' however, was most likely a *tholos* tomb, built like those at Mycenae of Cyclopean stone. The side chamber still retains its magnificent carved ceiling.

that the Dorians were there at least to end what others had begun. The Dorians were another Greek-speaking people, distant relatives of the Achaeans, who came down from the north – from Macedonia or possibly up in the Danube basin – a crude, backward people when they first appeared on Greek soil. The destruction of the leading Mycenaean palace-centers throughout the greater Aegean meant the collapse of the power that had kept this Greek world alert and alive. As power dissipated, pirates had the run of the sea, for instance, so trade and economic patterns were disrupted. By the time Mycenae was destroyed for the last time in about 1100 BC, the Mycenaean Bronze Age culture had already been irreparably tarnished. Some Mycenaeans fled from the Dorians, going off across the Aegean to the coast of Asia Minor and its offshore islands; while others seem to have pulled back into isolated pockets, Athens being one such. Meanwhile, those who remained throughout Greece became preoccupied with maintaining the basic elements of life and gave up many of the old skills and crafts. Nowhere was the loss more dramatic than in the plain fact that people totally forgot how to write Greek: the heroic glow of the Mycenaeans had dimmed and a dark age settled over the people of the Greek mainland and islands.

2. The Emergent Greeks

The concept or image of the 'Dark Age' that settled over Greece in the centuries following 1100 BC is one of those phrases like 'the cradle of civilization' that has undergone considerable modification in recent years. Like those terms once glibly applied to classical Athens, and indeed for many of the same reasons, this 'dark age' has come to be seen as a much more complex, multilayered and sophisticated period. No longer are the centuries between, say, 1100 and 800 BC dismissed as some 'black hole' of history into which the Mycenaean Greeks tumbled and out of which the Archaic Greeks suddenly emerged. No longer, in other words, is Greek culture seen as coming to an abrupt and absolute end, then lying virtually dormant for several centuries before suddenly flowering at a few centers. A darker age these centuries may have been in relation to the golden glow of Mycenae and the rosy dawn of Athens, but it is now generally recognized that there was far more continuity, far more interaction and far more culture than the phrase implies.

Although it is accepted that the apparent successors if not outright destroyers of the Mycenaean culture and centers were the Dorians, it would be misleading to imagine one monolithic group of Greeks replacing another monolithic group of Greeks throughout Greece. For one thing, the Dorians were probably only one of a number of Greek-speaking people living in the Balkan region who had remained pretty much untouched by the Achaean-Mycenaean Greek culture but who now moved down into Greece. These would include such groups now known by the regions of Greece that they took over – the Aetolians, Phocians, Locrians and others. Although the Dorians apparently ousted the Mycenaeans from their centers in many parts of Greece, they tended to concentrate their new forces and growth in the Peloponnesos – particularly the regions known as Laconia, Messenia and Argolis.

Again, though, none of these new peoples completely eliminated the previous peoples, Mycenaeans or others. In the interior of the Peloponnesos, for instance, in the region that would later achieve fame as Arcadia, the survival of the older population was evidenced by the language spoken by these Arcadians during later centuries. Other Mycenaeans seem to have moved into the mountainous region along the northern coast of the Peloponnesos, for that region would be known as Achaia in later times. Others seem to have retreated into Attica, where Mycenaeans had long settled – even the Acropolis of Athens had a Mycenaean citadel.

Still other Mycenaeans left the mainland, going to islands and lands to the east. Cyprus, for instance, had long attracted small groups of Mycenaean merchants and artisans, but about 1100 BC, a new wave of Mycenaeans seem to have established more permanent settlements there; the dialect spoken by the Greeks of Cyprus well into historical times is related to the Arcadian dialect, also regarded as a remnant of these same Mycenaeans. Some Mycenaean Greeks appear to have moved over to Cilicia, on the coast of Asia Minor. And there is a legend that descendants of Nestor of Pylos, one of the great Mycenaean centers, moved over to Miletus on the coast of Asia Minor. Still others – perhaps the original Mycenaeans of Athens and Attica or perhaps Mycenaeans who had spent some time there after first fleeing the invaders elsewhere in Greece – appeared on Aegean islands, particularly those just off the coast of Asia Minor, or along that coast itself. These Greeks are known as Aeolians and Ionians; in the next few centuries these Greeks would develop a prosperous and progressive culture known as Ionian, and in some respects they would prove to be ahead of the mainland Greeks.

According to later Greek legends and traditions, the Dorian invasion

Above: Three Protoattic vases with (*lower right*) two goblets and a covered box, or *pyxis*, in the Protocorinthian style of the late seventh century. The vase second from left typifies Near Eastern-inspired pottery, modeled partly in the shape of animal and/or human heads.

Right: A Protoattic vase depicting a wild-boar hunt in the top frieze. The sphinx-like figures below show the prevailing Eastern influence, but are still rendered very much in the Geometric manner (600–575 BC).

Previous pages: The Temple of Apollo at Corinth, built in the mid-sixth century BC, has several great monolithic columns still standing.

of the mainland occured about 1104 BC, an episode known as 'The Return of the Heraclidae,' a reference to the myth that the children of Herakles had been expelled from the Peloponnesos by King Eurystheus. Although modern archaeology can't pin such a major event down to such a simple date, the time-frame seems about right, and although the Mycenaean Greeks by no means just vanished from the scene, there is no denying that there was a relatively sharp discontinuity between Mycenaean and Dorian Greece. One change that occurred about this time, though, was that the people who inhabited Greece from this time on began to refer to themselves as 'Hellenes,' suggesting that they themselves were conscious of the communality of their culture.

But the fact remains that the Dorians seem to have possessed a rather basic material culture and relatively simple socio-political institutions. The Mycenaeans had already lost their old energy, but the Dorians were not the people to revitalize the Greeks overnight. The Greeks lost many if not most of their contacts with peoples outside Greece as life turned in on itself, focussed on basic subsistence at village level. Land once again became the prime measure of wealth and power – as opposed, say, to commercial transactions – and landed families evi-

Above: A lidded jar from Cyprus, its knob finished as an *amphora*.
Above left: A gold earring from Athens with patterns in wire and settings for inlays of glass or amber.
Right: The Temple of Apollo, the earliest Doric temple in Greece (mid-sixth century BC), against the Acrocorinth.

dently replaced the warrior-chieftains as the leaders of community life. To the extent that this cut down on the fighting that seems to have consumed so much of the energies of the Mycenaean Greeks, this was progress; but there was also a pettiness and provincialism to life at this time. There was probably a touch of paranoia: the world outside must have seemed rather threatening to the Greeks of this time.

Construction – at least of any permanent structures known today as worthy of the term 'architecture' – seemed to cease for several centuries. It was not that the Greeks of this period had no models: many of the Mycenaean structures, after all, were still standing: the Lion Gate of Mycenae could be admired throughout antiquity, and so many of the large stone walls and fortresses of the Mycenaeans were known that the Greeks attributed them to such shadowy predecessors as the Pelasgians and the Cyclopes. But the Greeks of these centuries did allow a dark age to settle over such skills as stone-cutting, seal engraving, ivory carving and metalworking.

One notable exception to this was in the skill – and even art – of pottery-making. Even in the decline of the Mycenaeans they had continued to make a pottery that is today classified as sub-Mycenaean – hardly among the most impressive works but nevertheless pottery was being made. And after all, clay vessels of one kind or another were among the basic necessities of life to the people of this time: metal was still far too scarce and expensive, glass was not available to Greeks of this time and containers made of wood or leather or textiles would soon perish. So it is the fired-clay pot or vase, practically indestructible even if it may be splintered, that survives to speak of the continuity of Greek culture across the centuries.

Perhaps it should be no surprise that some of the finest vases to appear in the earliest part of this 'dark age' came from Athens. Although Athens had not played much of a role in the Bronze Age culture of the Mycenaeans, her Acropolis had been the center of a settlement – and with the collapse of the Mycenaeans in the face of the Dorians or other newcomers, many of them seem to have gravitated to Athens and the Attic countryside. Starting sometime after 1100 BC, vase painters in Athens began to take such traditional hand-drawn Mycenaean patterns as arcs and circles and render them in a more precise fashion with compasses and comb-like brushes. This style of vase decoration which prevailed in much of the Greek world from about 1100 to 900 BC is now known as the Protogeometric style – simply a recognition that it anticipated the fully developed Geometric style that started in about 900 BC. The decoration of these Protogeometric vases consisted largely of concentric circles and semi-circles, diamonds, zigzags or wavy lines, usually arranged in horizontal bands around the vases. A fine black gloss paint was used, and although the early vases had most of their surface left unpainted, increasingly more of the vase surface came to be painted. The vases are well made and well proportioned, and if they now seem a bit austere they reflect the new Dorian spirit of no-nonsense orderliness.

This Protogeometric vase style spread from Athens throughout much of the then Greek world, but there is no suggestion that Athens was anything more than just one of many independent city-states or kingdoms. And there was not much else of artistic worth being made during these centuries in any part of the Greek world. No temples or public buildings, let alone domestic structures, have survived – they were probably made of wood or rubble or mud brick. Bronze safety pins (*fibulae*, as they are now called) have survived from burials. And there were clay human figurines being made, especially on Crete, where they seem to have been a continuation, however crude, of the Minoan tradition. Another type of ceramic of this period is the standing figure such

Above: A cinerary urn from Athens in the early Geometric style (*c* 900–850 BC).
Above right: A *fibula* (ornamental brooch) of the Boeotian type from the Geometric period, showing two figures conversing and a man attacked by a wolf.
Below right: A large *amphora* from the Dipylon Cemetery in Athens; the center panel shows the dead laid out on a bier, flanked by mourners.
Far right below: A Protogeometric *amphora* from Athens – mid- to late tenth century BC.

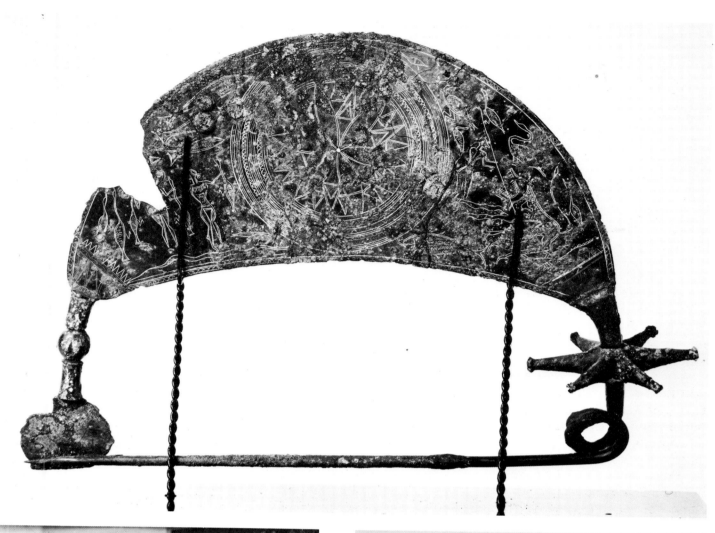

41

as a stag or some man-animal monster like a centaur or bull-man. Many of these figures were painted in the same manner as the Protogeometric vases, and some even were intended as vases; most seem to have been used as votive offerings or as tomb furnishings – that is, they were not designed for everyday use as pottery.

Then, about 900 BC and prevailing for another two centuries, there emerged the full Geometric style, exhibited in its most literal and consistent form by vase painting. Picking up the elements and design of the Protogeometric style, the new vase painters added still more geometric elements – meanders, swastikas, triangles – and instead of confining the decoration to a few limited areas of a vase, they began to cover the entire vessel with the patterns in their horizontal bands. Formerly blank spaces between the bands were now filled with strips of simple elements. And by about 800 BC, vase painters also began to use figures to decorate the surfaces; initially these were only animals – horses, deer, birds – and they were clearly present simply as decorative motifs, almost reduced to their own geometric-abstract forms. By 750 BC, human figures began to appear but were again treated as geometric forms, with little or no attempt at any realistic observation of detail.

Very quickly, though, these human figures not only began to be shown with individualistic elements – warriors are distinguished by helmets, women mourners are seen tearing their hair – but also the human figures were shown in scenes of action: bodies are being carried to the cemetery, warriors duel. Although most of these scenes were taken from everyday life – hunting, fighting, dancing – others clearly depicted episodes involving the individuals of Greek myth and legend –

Above: Terracotta of women kneading dough.
Below: A Bronze-Age cauldron.

Above: An Attic *aryballos* (perfume flask), *c* seventh century.

Herakles fighting the lion, Odysseus shipwrecked, well-known combats at Troy.

And it is no coincidence that it was at this time that Homer was also gathering in the age-old oral traditions about the Trojan War and the subsequent wanderings of Odysseus before fashioning them into the *Iliad* and the *Odyssey*. And the attribution of these epic poems to this one great bard also fits in with another phenomenon of this time – say, about 750 BC – namely, the development of writing among the Greeks. The old, relatively primitive forms of culture were giving way to newer, more sophisticated forms, drawing upon the traditional but looking ahead to the innovative.

Athens, once more, seems to have taken the lead in these Geometric vases, but other Greek cities were soon following – and if they did not all attempt the more elaborate scenes of the Late Geometric Athenian vase paintings, neither did they slavishly imitate the Athenians. Meanwhile, the style of the Geometric vases was also being used on other works made by Greeks in these centuries – incised on the *fibulae*, or safety pins, or carved on sealstones. Freestanding bronze or clay figures in the round often seemed to match the figures on Geometric vases, and there were clearly many shared motifs – hunters, warriors and animals. Most of these figures have been found at sanctuaries at places such as Athens, Samos, Olympia, Delphi or Dodona, and by the end of the 8th century some of these figures were inscribed with the name of the donor, recipient (deity) and even the reason for the offering: clearly a sense of the individual, a tinge of self-consciousness, had emerged among the Greeks in a wide area.

For indeed, during these last two hundred or so years, the period denoted by art historians as the Geometric, many more changes had been occurring in Greece than just these elaborations of vase paintings. As suggested by the consolidation of the old myths and legends and tales in the Homeric epics, the Greeks of this period were developing a consciousness of their shared culture and goals. As the historian Herodotus would put it some three centuries later, the Greeks of this time were becoming aware of 'being of the same stock and the same speech,' of having 'common shrines of the gods and common rivals.'

With this emergent consciousness came a certain dissatisfaction with the status quo. Much of the best and most accessible land had been falling into the hands of an élite who were increasing their political as well as economic control over the less fortunate masses. This minority of wealthy and powerful families would then grant credit to the poorer farmers – far and away the majority of people were still farming or herding – until they became so indebted as to be almost serfs. The emergence of different socio-economic classes ran counter to the traditional tribal organization of the Greeks, which had been rather more egalitarian, involving as it did common property, exchange and barter of produce and products and a sense of mutual solidarity. Whether because of this economic pressure or because the population was simply increasing, more and more people were unable to live off the land and they had to turn elsewhere for subsistence. This meant that they moved into towns and ports where there were activities that could provide some pay for their labor, and cities began to grow – still small in today's terms, but definitely cities in the social and economic sense.

One of the main activities in these growing rural and port towns was commerce, both in the trade of basic food and raw materials produced by Greeks or their neighbors and in the trade in more exotic luxury items. These latter items were now beginning to be traded throughout the eastern Mediterranean, particularly by the Phoenicians and other peoples along the coasts of the Levant and Asia Minor, who in many respects were more advanced than the Greeks of this time. By 800 BC, merchants from Euboea, the large island just off the northeast shoulder of Attica, as well as from the Aegean islands, were sailing to the eastern coast of the Mediterranean; one of their trading stations was at the mouth of the Orontes River (then in northern Syria, now part of Turkey) at a site known as Al Mina; Cypriot Greeks were already trading there, for it was an ideal link between the Mediterranean and Mesopotamia, and these new Greek merchant-adventurers soon crowded out the Cypriots.

Up and down the coast, similar groups of Greek traders were setting up trading stations – and as they did, they began to ship back to Greece numerous new objects that were made or decorated in ways quite different from the prevailing Geometric style. There were bronze bowls, for instance, with low relief scenes of animals and human figures; ivory plaques carved in low relief; hammered metalwork and new types of cauldrons and a new repertoire of monsters to represent in sculpture or depict on vases. These new materials – new to this era of Greeks at least – techniques and designs soon began to be adopted and adapted by Greek artisans and artists, and because of the Eastern origins of such work, this period, approximately 700–600 BC, is known as the Orientalizing Style.

In some places, this new style seems to have been brought over to Greek locales by foreign craftsmen; on Crete, in particular, there were families or studios of immigrant craftsmen who introduced new techniques such as hammering bronze over wooden cores to make sculptured figures or hammered bronze shields, while in Athens and Attica immi-

Above: A decorative motif from Corinth in the Orientalizing style, which introduced floral designs and figurative representations to Greek art. The Corinthians readily adapted Eastern influences to their artistic needs.

Below: A Cycladic jug in the early Protocorinthian style featuring a gryphon's head – found on the island of Aegina. Potters of the Cyclades Islands commonly modeled vases in the shape of animals.

Right: Detail of a Geometric vase from the period when Greek artists began to admit figure decoration as an element of design. By the mid-ninth century BC, both human and animal figures were being depicted, still with Geometric economy of detail. Single panels like this one would later be extended into a frieze.

Below: A wine jug (*oinochoë*) typical of the Corinthian figure-painted pottery that was exported widely in the sixth century BC, until Athenian wares took over the markets.

Above: A Corinthian wine jug in the more miniaturist style that recalls the Protocorinthian.

grant goldsmiths were making new types of jewelry. But the most pervasive and persistent effect of this new style was, not unexpectedly, on the vases, where native Greek potters had their own traditions to build upon. As they began to see more of these new works from such lands as Egypt, Assyria and Phoenicia, the Greek potters moved on from strict geometric designs and austere shapes. They began to paint new designs such as floral motifs, lotus flowers and palmettes; they used more color, and broke away from the orderly horizontal bands; lions, panthers and sphinxes replaced the traditional deer, goats and horses; human figures were no longer depicted as abstract geometric silhouettes but with more realism; even the shapes of the vases began to take life, for some were made to look like griffins and other animals or even humans.

Still another development distinguishes the Orientalizing style of vase painting: with the growing diversification of Greek society and the Greek world in general, various city-states and locales began to develop their own variations of the basic style, variations that reflected their own local traditions. Athens, for instance, adopted the Orientalizing style but because of its deep commitment to the Geometric style, the Athenian potters were somewhat more conservative than Greek potters in other locales. The figures and floral patterns taken over from the East were treated in the Geometric manner, for instance, in what is now known as the Protoattic style. But at Corinth, with less of a tradition of figure drawing, the potters were quicker to adopt the new Orientalizing style of floral designs and figurative representations. In particular, the Corinthian vase painters devised a new technique, drawing figures with black paint but incising details with thin clear lines so that the lighter clay showed through; this is known as the 'black-figured' style, and along with the other distinctive elements employed by the Corinthian potters of the time between about 725–625 BC makes up what is known as the Protocorinthian style.

This new spirit of experimentation and diversity was by no means confined to such major cities as Athens and Corinth. On the Aegean islands, Greek vase painters were quick to adopt a polychromatic style that had started in Athens. On such islands as Crete and Aegina, potters modelled vases in the shape of animals or human heads. The Athenian-Attic style of drawing was adopted by some of the Peloponnesian vase painters, and the island of Melos also adapted the Attic styles of drawing and polychrome. Meanwhile, the Greeks of the islands and cities along the coast of Asia Minor – known as Ionia – and also on Rhodes took up a decorative style that employed friezes of animals (the most common being the wild goat, which has since given its name to the style). Some of these styles were clearly rooted in the indigenous Geometric tradition, while others looked to foreign and Eastern influences – but all were now part of the expanding possibilities for Greeks of the eighth and seventh centuries BC.

By this time, the Greeks were progressing far beyond the confines of the 'dark age' and had emerged as a true political and cultural presence in the Eastern Mediterranean. The Ionian Greeks along the coast and offshore islands of Asia Minor were particularly progressive

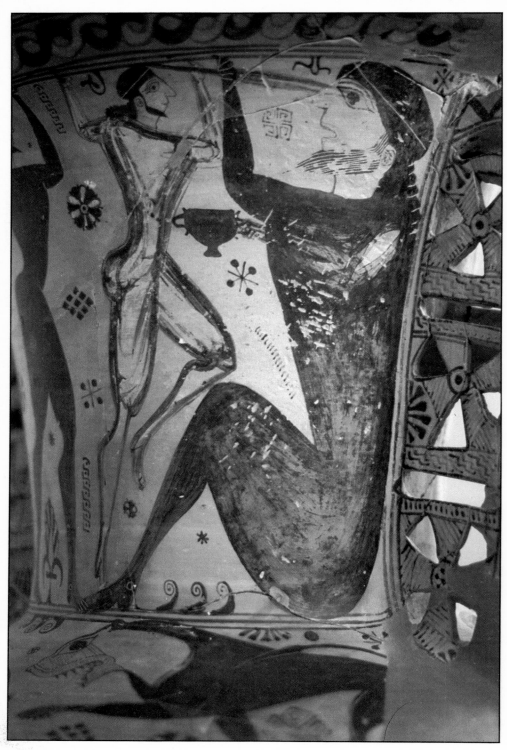

Left: Detail of a Protoattic vase dating from about 650 BC showing the blinding of Polyphemus. The stick-like figure at left harks back to the Geometric style, as contrasted with the more lifelike renditions of the other two figures.
Right: An ivory relief depicting two women who may be the daughters of Proitos; they were driven mad by Hera and ranged over the countryside attacking wayfarers (650–625 BC).

and expansive in their maritime commerce. But Greeks from many locales had been migrating around much of the Mediterranean since the middle of the eighth century BC – in part because of the shortage of arable land, which led to a concentration of economic and political power in narrowing circles, but also because of a new spirit of enterprise. Greek colonists were now settled as far west as the coast of Spain and its offshore Balearic Islands, along the North African coast, in many parts of Sicily and southern Italy, up into Thrace and even around the Black Sea; Greeks were even permitted to set up a major trading settlement in Egypt, at Naucratis on the Nile Delta.

Wherever the Greeks were settling, they brought much of their own culture with them, but they were also quick to learn from the foreigners. From the Phoenicians, for instance, the Greeks adopted an alphabet about 750 BC and were soon adapting it for their own language. And from the Lydians of western Asia Minor the Greeks of about a century later were adopting the practice of striking coins. Both these new 'tools' opened up tremendous new opportunities to all kinds of people: by facilitating communication and commerce, they helped to unsettle some of the old conservative landowners and power-brokers. They also contributed to the growth of the *polis*, literally a city but more like a city-state in the geographical and political extent of its power. The *polis* during the 600s was far from a democracy, however; large groups of people had no citizenship – in particular, women, but also slaves and non-nativeborn Greeks. The real power lay in the hands of men who could trace their descent to traditional tribes, but there was also growing friction between the old landed aristocrats and the new generations who were advancing through commerce.

This development was especially clear at Corinth, situated at the isthmus that was a major crossroad for much of the traffic of the Greek world. One of the oldest tribes, or *gens*, of Corinth was the Bacchidae (a name derived from Bacchus, whom they claimed as their progenitor), members of which began to engage in trading during the eighth century BC. And in 747 BC, the hereditary kings of Corinth lost their power to members of the Bacchidae *gens*, who were now taking the lead in promoting trade and colonization. And because Corinth was in the vanguard of the other Greek city-states in its economic activities, social tensions also came to a head sooner than elsewhere. Out of this social and economic ferment arose the first *tyrannos*, or tyrant.

A tyrant at this time was not necessarily what this term has since come to mean. The term referred to men who were able to gain power without appealing to either hereditary rights or traditional prestige. A tyrant, rather, seemed to be able to interpret the needs of the people and then gain almost absolute power by satisfying the will of the majority – at least the majority of male citizens who might have enjoyed any power. A tyrant provided strong leadership in such areas as foreign relations, public works and cultural support, and to that extent was a benevolent leader.

The first tyrant of Corinth was Cypselus, a member of the Bacchidae, who assumed power in 657 BC. For some 30 years, Cypselus would provide strong leadership for Corinth and help it to maintain its lead in trade and colonization. Then in 629 BC, his son Periander took over, and he would rule for 44 years, leading Corinth to still greater heights of prosperity and power. Periander, for instance, reconquered the island of Kerkyra (Corfu) off the west coast of Greece and a crucial base for all ships passing between Greece and Sicily or other points to the west. (Corinth had already set up a colony at Syracuse in Sicily in 734 BC.) And it was typical of such a tyrant as Periander that one of the things he did to win over the natives of Kerkyra was to order the erection of a

Top right: The Code of Gortyn, Crete, a series of municipal laws formulated in 500 BC and written *boustrophedon* (as the plough-ox turns): each alternate line – for the reader – runs from right to left.
Below right: An eighteenth-century print of the Temple of Apollo at Corinth.
Below: The Doric Temple of Apollo Epikourios at Bassae, in the Peloponnese, attributed to Iktinus, the architect of the Parthenon (second half of the fifth century BC).

Temple of Artemis, one of the earliest examples of monumental Greek architecture. For in setting himself up above the old aristocratic and tribal authorities, a tyrant turned to monumental buildings to express this new power of the state.

Periander was succeeded briefly by his nephew Psammetikos, but he was soon overthrown by an oligarchy of merchants; they authorized the construction of the Temple of Apollo – which, like the Temple of Artemis on Kerkyra, the Temple of Hera at Olympia and the Temple of Apollo at Delphi, was one of the earliest and finest of the great temples on the Greek mainland. Already the architects and craftsmen were employing subtle techniques to compensate for the distortions that the human eye perceives when looking at absolutely straight lines: for instance, because the *stylobate*, or foundation level, would appear to sag slightly under the mass of the columns and upper structure, it was made to curve slightly higher at the center. It would be another century before even the Athenians would introduce such sophisticated devices into their buildings.

Elsewhere throughout Greece, other people were also advancing in their own ways during the sixth century BC. The homeland of the Aetolians, along the west-central region of the mainland, was well off the main routes of Greek commerce but this did not prevent them participating, in their own way, in the pan-Hellenic culture. The Aetolians' religious center was at Thermon, near Lake Trichonis, where they held an annual festival at which they elected their ruling magistrates. And it was at Thermon that the Aetolians erected their own Temple of Apollo in the sixth century, hardly a major temple but still a testament to the Greek influence. Over on Crete, the Dorians had been settled for many centuries and had developed their own society and culture, with its capital – or at least main center – at Gortyn, near the old Minoan

Left: The sacred pool at Thermon, used for religious rites of purification.
Below right: Fragment of the temple complex to Hera (the Heraeum) on the Sporades island of Samos, which was a great maritime power in the fifth century BC.
Below: The Heraeum was the work of the architect Rhoikos and was considered the largest Greek temple of its time (sixth century BC).

center of Phaestos by the south-central coast. By the end of the sixth century, Gortyn was so advanced that it had one of the most detailed law codes of the day inscribed on stone blocks.

On Samos, another island at an opposite edge of the Aegean, still another community of Greeks was prospering. Samos had been settled by Ionians at the time of the Dorians' arrival on the mainland, and by 650 BC was such an advanced maritime power that one of the islanders, Kolaios, seems to have voyaged all the way through the Pillars of Herakles – the Strait of Gibraltar. By about 540 BC, Polycrates and his two brothers took over from the ruling landed aristocracy, but Polycrates soon pushed out his brothers and assumed sole command as a tyrant. Under Polycrates, Samos built up its naval fleet, annexed some of its neighboring islands, made alliances with other powers around the Mediterranean, and founded colonies from Sicily in the west to the Sea of Marmara in the northeast. Polycrates attracted artists and poets such as Theodoros and Anacreon to his court and authorized the construction of three works that Herodotus regarded as the greatest to be seen anywhere in Greece: the great mole of the harbor (at modern Pithagorio); the aqueduct that was cut through a mountain under the direction of the architect Eupalinos; and the great Temple to Hera, built by the architect Rhoikos (aided by Theodoros) and considered the largest Greek temple of its time.

Closer to the mainland there was yet another thriving Greek community on the island of Aegina, southwest of Athens in the Saronic Gulf. Because of its restricted arable land, Aegina had been quick to turn to the sea and trade, and it prospered particularly by bringing grain from Egypt to the cities of central Greece and in exchange giving Egyptians silver from its mines. Aegina had been one of the first Greek city-states to mint its own coins, sometime about 665 BC; the coins were manufactured in the shape of tortoises to reflect the approximate shape

Above: The head of a youth with hair tied back in a club style – fragment of a grave *stele* of the Archaic period (*c* 560 BC).
Far left: Shaft drums still standing at the Heraeum show the column construction technique that succeeded the monolithic (single-shaft) style. Several stone drums were mortared together, or anchored through the center by a shaft driven into the ground.
Left: The gravestone of Aristion, signed by the artist Aristocles, showing the uniform of a *hoplite* or heavy infantryman. Originally the background was painted red, and the figure still bears traces of red and blue paint.

of the island, and the silver *chelonai* ('tortoises') of Aegina were widely accepted among other commercial states. The people of Aegina were of Dorian stock and thus were regarded by the Athenians as more than just commercial rivals; indeed, when Darius' Persians came to challenge the Athenians in 491 BC and were threatened by a storm, Aegina would provide refuge for the Persians. And by about 495 BC, the Aeginans were engaged in building one of the greatest of all the early Greek temples, dedicated to Aphaea, an ancient local goddess, which boasted some of the finest sculpture of the time in its pediments.

The sculpture for the Temple of Aphaea on Aegina represents the culmination of the work of a century or more for Greek artists working in various forms, a period now designated as the Archaic. Like all periods or styles, it did not commence abruptly at the start of one century, let alone with one year or artist, but by about 600 BC the Archaic style appears to have pervaded the Greek world. Drawing upon the foreign influences that had been so evident in the previous Orientalizing style, the Archaic artists and artisans now seemed to have found a more authentic and less artificial Greek voice. Sculpture, for instance, had for some time been under the influence of Egyptian and Assyrian traditions, with a certain stiffness, aloofness and schematization. But Greek sculptors, beginning on Crete with the so-called Daedalic style, began to free themselves from these formal conventions and were depicting the human form in ways that were both truer to the anatomical realities and more expressive of human ideals. Vase painters were also experimenting with a variety of techniques such as the red-figured style that appeared about 530 BC, and the paintings were now done with a

The Doric Temple of Aphaia on the island of Aegina. The goddess was a local deity who had affinities with Artemis. Sculpture on both the west and east pediments depicts scenes from the Trojan Wars.

confidence and flair that made the simplest vase a work of art. The Archaic style was also adopted by artisans working with ivory, gold, gemstones and glass, and Greek painters were now painting both wooden panels and frescoed walls with a recognizable Archaic style.

Greeks were now united by a certain style in their arts and crafts – temples from Sicily to Asia Minor looked very similar, vases recognized as Greek could be found in use throughout the Mediterranean and much sculpture throughout the Greek world represented figures with a distinctive 'Archaic smile' – yet there was by no means political unity or harmony among the Greeks in the political sense. Both among the mother-cities and in their farflung colonies, there was increasing rivalry and even outright hostility, of which that between Athens and Aegina was only one manifestation. Since the coming of the Dorians, the Greeks had had over 600 years in which to form some kind of pan-Hellenic political institution, but they had failed to do so. Instead, by 490 BC they were on the verge of a series of conflicts that would eventually lead to their political disintegration.

Above: Polyphemus and Odysseus on a vase fragment from Argos in the Argive shape. The drawing resembles Attic work, while the washes of paint on the human bodies are typical of island vases (mid-seventh century BC).
Right: A terracotta figurine of the late sixth century BC: 'The Cooking Lesson.' Terracotta was often used as the medium for homely scenes from everyday life.

3. The Great Sanctuaries: Delphi and Olympia

The Greeks lived in a multitude of small city-states, independent political entities frequently at odds with one another. Even in times of peace, there was much that divided neighboring city-states: each city had its own coinage, dialect and local deities. Yet all these 'Greeks' spoke Greek, and all worshipped the Olympian deities. Whatever the local cult or the local shrine, all Greeks worshipped Zeus, and all Greeks looked to a handful of important shrines such as Delphi and Olympia. Although there were other important shrines (Dodona, for example) by the eighth century, Delphi was the pan-Hellenic oracle *par excellence*. And although there were other important festival and game centers (Isthmia, for example), Olympia early took pride of place as the seat of the most important pan-Hellenic games.

Previous pages: The Temple of Apollo, the great shrine at Delphi, overlooks the valley of the Pleistos.

Right: The *Omphalos*, the great stone which covered a cleft in the rocks near the great altar at Delphi, was considered the center of the world by the ancient Greeks.

Far left: The Sphinx, a mythical creature with a lion's body, eagle's wings and a woman's head, was dedicated by the people of Naxos and stood on a column behind the Rock of the Sibyl at Delphi.
Above left: One of the wonders of ancient Delphi that is now visible is the remarkable drainage system.
Left: The Siphnian Treasury at Delphi has caryatids instead of the more familiar Ionic columns.

DELPHI

The ancient Greeks believed that Delphi was the center of the world and sacred to the god Apollo, whose oracle and sanctuary were here. Delphi's physical beauty is so overwhelming that it is easy to understand why the ancients thought it must be a sacred spot. Delphi combines the common elements of Greek landscape – sea, mountains, olive trees – in an uncommon setting. The shrine is between two massive cliffs known as the Phaedriades (the Shining Ones), which reflect the first beams of sunrise and the last rays at sunset. The cliffs are outcroppings at the base of Mount Parnassos, which rises 8200 feet above the olive-clad Pleistos Valley. In fact, Delphi is on the only pass north through the Parnassos range into central and northwest Greece. The religious shrine and sanctuary grew up at the spot where the narrow, winding pass widens, forming a natural amphitheater.

It was not merely the great natural beauty of the site which caused the Greeks to build here: evidently there was a chasm in the earth whence mysterious vapors issued, inspiring some with the gift of prophecy. The chasm was believed to be on the exact spot where two eagles, released at opposite ends of the earth by Zeus, met. Thus Delphi was the *omphalos*, or navel, of the earth: its exact center.

Previous pages: The theater at Delphi, at the top of the Sacred Way, was used for sacred dramas. Below the circular stage can be seen the ruined Temple of Apollo.
Left: The Temple of Apollo at Delphi was built in the sixth century BC.

Right: The stones of the temple of Apollo were held together by bronze ligatures. Most of these have been removed.

Above: Mount Parnassus, sacred to the gods, rises behind the Temple of Apollo at Delphi.
Left: The Athenian Stoa below the Temple of Apollo. In the foreground stands a column drum with an Ionic capital.

The legend of the two eagles is but one of many which surround Delphi. The second century AD traveller Pausanias remarked when he visited Delphi that 'There are many contradictory stories about Delphi, and many more about Apollo's oracle.' According to some of these stories, first the earth goddess Ge was worshipped here, then the sea god Poseidon and finally the Apollo, god of prophecy.

The Homeric Hymn to Apollo records many of the legends surrounding Apollo and Delphi, and the Greek poets and playwrights told these stories over and over again. In addition, Greek artists showed Apollo's exploits on vases and on the sculptured reliefs of temples. In some of these legends, the young Apollo slew a fearful serpent (the Python) at Delphi, in its lair beside the Castalian Spring which bubbles out of a cleft below Apollo's sanctuary.

The Greeks believed that Apollo was the god of reason, associated with all the rational and civilizing forces of progress including music, prophecy, law and the expansion of Greek culture overseas through colonies. Apollo's victory over the red-eyed Python was therefore seen by the Greeks as symbolic of their own victory over the forces of darkness and primitivism.

After Apollo slew the Python, he left Delphi in self-imposed exile as punishment for the murder, righteous though it was. After eight years, Apollo returned, and found that where the Python had once held sway there was now a Pythia, a priestess gifted with the gift of prophecy. According to some legends, Apollo himself built the first temple at Delphi, and thereafter spoke through the Pythia at the oracle.

In yet other legends, Apollo came first to Delphi in the guise of a dolphin, swimming into the Gulf of Corinth and bringing with him a shipload of Cretans to serve as his priests. Some believed that the dolphin took its name (*delphini* in Greek) from the town of Delphi because of Apollo's visit there. In still other legends, Apollo first came to Delphi from the north, striding down through the beautiful Vale of Tempe in Thessaly. At Tempe, Apollo paused to gather some laurel — and forever after, victors in the Pythian Games held every four years at Delphi were crowned with laurel from Tempe.

As Pausanias remarked, the stories about Apollo are many and contradictory. The myths say that the first shrine at Delphi was to the primitive earth goddess Ge, and there was a sanctuary and a small village at Delphi in the Mycenaean period (fourteenth to eleventh

centuries BC). During the Geometric Period (eleventh to ninth centuries BC), the cult of Apollo was established, reflecting the belief that the god of reason had vanquished other deities at Delphi.

By the Archaic Period (750–550 BC), Delphi was *the* important shrine in Greece. No Greek city planning to establish a colony overseas did so without first seeking Delphi's advice as to the best site. When the colony flourished, the grateful townspeople sent thank-offerings back to Delphi. In this way, the sanctuary grew in wealth and splendor. The Sacred Way, which ran through the sanctuary and past the Temple of Apollo, was lined with more than 20 treasuries, elegantly constructed marble buildings housing lavish dedications of gold, silver and precious works of art.

Naturally, the most powerful city-states built the most splendid treasuries. The island of Siphnos, rich in gold, attempted to outshine all the other treasuries with its Ionic temple, decorated with a sculptured frieze. When the Siphnians ceased to send tribute to Delphi, an angry Apollo flooded their gold mines and the island lost its source of wealth.

After their great victory over the Persians at the Battle of Marathon, the Athenians dedicated one-tenth of the victory spoils to build their treasury at Delphi. The sculptured frieze which ran around the treasury commemorated the victories of the legendary Athenian hero Theseus. The walls of the treasury and its retaining wall served as giant notice boards, as visitors inscribed dedications, honors and even entire hymns to Apollo on the smooth stones.

Bottom : The Athenians built a temple to the tutelary goddess of their city at Delphi.
Below : The familiar egg and dart molding carved around a column base at Delphi.

Every city-state which could build a treasury at Delphi did so, and sometimes old enemies found themselves as neighbors on the Sacred Way. The Syracusans, for example, delighted in building their treasury directly across from the treasury of the Athenians, whom they had just defeated in one of the critical battles of the Peloponnesian War.

City-states which could not afford to build a treasury instead erected a statue along the Sacred Way, with the result that every available inch was soon taken up with statues of statesmen and heroes, gods and goddesses. There were statues of goats and bulls, of athletes and heroes, as well as dedications of weapons. There were so many statues that when the Roman emperor Nero visited Delphi, he could cart off 500 and still leave behind such famous works as the Charioteer of Delphi, the Naxian Sphinx and the colossal statues of the youths Cleobis and Biton.

Whereas individual cities dedicated treasuries and statues, all the city-states (and several foreign powers) contributed funds for the Temple to Apollo. Legend has it that Apollo himself built the first temple out of laurel branches he had gathered in the Vale of Tempe, and that his disciples built a second temple out of beeswax and feathers. By the Archaic Period, a massive Doric temple stood on one of the few level spots in the sanctuary, its foundations supported by a powerful retaining wall. The roof and pediment were of Parian marble, and admonitions such as 'Know Thyself' and 'Nothing in Excess' were carved above the temple doorway.

To this spot came all who wished to consult the oracle, whether king or commoner. Inside, seated on a tripod, over the mysterious chasm, inhaling the mantic vapors, sat the Priestess. Initially, the Priestess prophesied but once a year, but as Delphi's popularity grew almost daily seances were held.

Often what the Priestess said was unintelligible to her audience, and on these occasions the temple priests interpreted Apollo's message. Even when the Pythia spoke clearly, her message was often ambiguous. When the fabulously rich Lydian king Croesus asked the oracle whether he should attack Greece, the Priestess replied that he would destroy a great kingdom if he did so. Encouraged, Croesus attacked – only to

Previous pages: Page 66: The Charioteer of Delphi, one of the few surviving free-standing bronze statues, was discovered in a pile of rubble on the north side of the Temple of Apollo.
Page 67: The figure of the Sphinx was also used on grave *stelae*. Like most marble statuary of the Classic period, this one was highly painted.

Right: The gryphon is another Near Eastern mythical beast whose form appears often in Greek art. This bronze decorated a cauldron.
Bottom: Many of the Greek city-states built small temples and treasuries within the sacred precincts of Delphi.

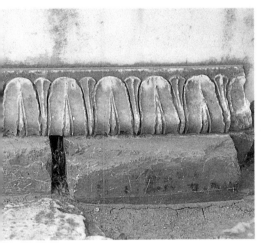

Above: The Stadium at Delphi, high above the temple precincts, was the site of games during the Pythian Festival.
Far left: The starting line for the runners at the stadium at Delphi.
Left: Ionic columns were topped by capitals with a scroll or volute on either side.
Right: The three standing columns of the Temple of Athena Pronaos at Delphi still carry elements of the architrave and frieze above them.

discover that the kingdom he destroyed was his own. On earlier occasions, Croesus had been better served by the oracle and had given one of the shrine's most lavish thank-offerings, a monumental silver bull.

As the philosopher Heraclitus (ca. 500 BC) said, the oracle 'neither conceals nor reveals the truth, but only hints at it.' When the Athenians in 480 BC asked Delphi how best to withstand the Persian invasion, the oracle instructed Athens to put her faith in her wooden wall. Only the Athenian leader Themistocles realized that the oracle did not mean the defensive wall around the city but the wooden ships of Athens's great fleet. Consequently, Themistocles marshalled Athens's fleet and decisively defeated the Persians in the naval battle off Salamis. After trouncing the Persian fleet, the Athenians pursued their enemy as far as the Hellespont, where they seized the massive cables of the bridge the Persian Emperor Xerxes had constructed to cross from Asia into Europe. The Athenians dedicated these cables at Delphi, and hung them on the massive polygonal wall beneath the Temple of Apollo.

Although Delphi was uniquely Apollo's, he was not the only deity whom the Greeks honored there. In the lower sanctuary, near the lovely round *tholos*, a mysterious cult building of unknown purpose, the

The treasury of the Athenians, built in 490 BC, stood at a turn in the Sacred Way to the Temple of Apollo.

Beyond the Athenian Treasury with its Doric columns stood the Rock of the Sibyl.

Greeks built two temples to Athena. In addition, a temple to the earth goddess Ge was maintained nearby not far from the Rock of the Sibyl, where the Sibyl Herophine spoke in riddles of the future. Pausanias said that the Sibyl was the daughter of a mortal and a nymph, 'born between man and goddess, daughter of sea monsters and immortal nymph.' Some believed that she was the sister of Apollo himself, others that she was his daughter. In short, although Apollo was the lord of Delphi, he shared his sanctuary with all the gods, just as all the Greeks shared in Delphi itself.

The presence of the oracle alone would have made Delphi unique and powerful in the Greek world, but every four years Delphi was the site of the Pythian games. During the games, the sanctuary was even more crowded than usual as athletes and their supporters poured into Delphi from all over the Greek world. Even wars were halted so that athletes and spectators could have safe passage to Delphi.

During the games, there were performances in the theater, hewn from local limestone, with elegant seats of local Parnassian marble. Here the revels in honor of Dionysus took place in front of 5000 spectators. Yet higher on the slopes of the sanctuary was the stadium, where 7000 spectators could watch runners speed from the starting line around the course. Here, too, the Charioteer of Delphi would have urged his team of four horses on to victory in the home stretch.

As the oracle's prestige grew, so grew the sanctuary, and control of Delphi gradually seemed too important to leave to the inhabitants of the little mountain village. The Greeks fought a series of wars, known as the Sacred Wars, as first powerful neighbors and then distant powers sought to gain control of Delphi and its oracle. Finally Philip of Macedon, father of Alexander the Great, seized and held the shrine, along with most of Greece itself.

Although visitors still came to Delphi, after Philip's victory, the oracle was no longer viewed as the center of the Greek world. When great leaders visited, all too often they came, like Nero, for plunder. When the last pagan emperor, Julian the Apostate (360–63 AD), sent a messenger to consult the oracle, back came its last known message: 'Go tell the King, the well-wrought hall has fallen in the dust; Phoebus Apollo no longer has a home or laurel, or a murmuring spring. Even the talkative spring has dried up and is no more.'

OLYMPIA

All the Greeks shared in the Oracle of Delphi, just as they shared in the Olympic Festivals. Both Delphi and Olympia were pan-Hellenic shrines, where Greeks from Macedonia in the north and Laconia in the south, from the colonies of Asia Minor and the far-flung islands, met together. Delphi had visitors every day, as did Olympia, but every fourth year from 776 BC to 393 AD Olympia was thronged with visitors to the Olympic Games. For the period of the games (held in the late summer) a pan-Hellenic truce came into effect, as with the Pythian Games at Delphi. All hostilities in the Greek world ceased, so that athletes could travel safely to the sanctuary to compete. The prize – a simple wreath of wild olive shoots – was valued more than all the gold of Croesus.

As with virtually every place of significance to the Greeks, Olympia's beginnings were explained by various myths. Some believed that the first contest held at Olympia was the competition to win the hand of the maiden Hippodameia, the beautiful daughter of King Oinomaos. Oinomaos did not wish his daughter to marry (some say because he loved her himself, others say because he feared that he would be killed by a son of Hippodameia). The shrewd king set up a contest for Hippodameia's many suitors which he was sure that he could win. Oinomaos, a superb horseman, challenged each of the suitors to a chariot race; the winner was to get Hippodameia, the loser was to die.

Over the years, Oinomaos met, defeated and killed 13 suitors, and Hippodameia was resigning herself to a life of spinsterhood when the hero Pelops appeared. Pelops had already survived dangers greater than a mere chariot race: when only a child, his father Tantalus had cooked him and served him up in a stew to the Olympian gods. Tantalus had been attempting to trick the gods, and to prove that they could eat human flesh unknowingly. Indeed, the goddess Demeter *did* take one bite from young Pelops's shoulder, but instantly recognized her mistake. Pelops was saved, and the gods gave him an ivory shoulder to replace the one which Demeter had inadvertently eaten.

In any event, when Pelops came seeking Hippodameia's hand in marriage, he knew of the 13 ill-fated suitors who had already met their deaths attempting to outrace King Oinomaos. Shrewdly, if not honorably, Pelops bribed Oinomaos' charioteer to loosen the linch-pins of his master's chariot; when Pelops and Oinomaos raced, Oinomaos' chariot wheels came off, the king was thrown and killed and Pelops married Hippodameia. In the hopes of keeping secret his victory stratagem, Pelops killed the king's charioteer, Myrtilus, and threw the body into a part of the Aegean which became known as the Myrtoan Sea after the disloyal servant.

Pelops and Hippodameia had six sons, and the fortunes of their family seemed assured. As was so often the case in Greek mythology, however, this was not to be: from Pelops and Hippodameia descended the ill-fated house of Atreus, whose most famous member, Agamemnon, was killed by his cousin Aegisthus. Still, Pelops himself gave his name to the Peloponnese ('Pelops' island'), and the Greeks chose to show the chariot race of Pelops and Oinomaos on the east pediment of the majestic Temple of Zeus at Olympia.

According to yet other legends, the race of Pelops and Oinomaos was not the origin of the Olympic games. Some Greeks believed that Herakles himself founded the games to celebrate his own success in completing the famous 12 labors, six of which he performed in the Peloponnese. The last labor was cleansing the foul stables of King Augeas of Elis, which

Above: The entrance to the Stadium at Olympia, where the ancient Olympic Games were first held in 776 BC.

Right: The classic sanctuary at Olympia grew up around a cult place of the older religion, centering on the worship of the Mother Goddess.

Herakles did by damming the River Alpheios and diverting it so that it ran through the filthy stableyards. Many Greeks believed that the sanctuary of Olympia grew up where the stableyards and palace had been, and the labors of Herakles were therefore commemorated in a series of sculptured panels in the sanctuary.

However the games were founded, they were held in honor of Zeus – the greatest of all the Olympian gods – at the sanctuary of Olympia, in the meadows where the rivers Alpheios and Kladeos meet. One's admiration for the contestants doubles when it is realized that the games were held between mid-August and mid-September, when the river valley can be oppressively hot and – unusual for Greece – humid. Nonetheless, the end of the summer marked the completion of the harvest – and, with the harvest safely in, most Greeks could rest, relax and enjoy the games, although both the heat and the crowds could be overwhelming.

The second century AD philosopher Epictetus said of the games, 'There are enough irksome and troublesome things in life; aren't things just as bad at the Olympic festival? Aren't you scorched there by the fierce heat? Aren't you crushed in the crowd? Isn't it difficult to freshen yourself up? Doesn't the rain soak you to the skin? Aren't you bothered by the noise, the din and the other nuisances? But it seems to me that you are well able to bear and indeed gladly endure all this, when you think of the gripping spectacles that you will see.'

The Olympic games lasted five days, with the different sports events held during the daytime and orations, religious celebrations and banquets taking up the evenings. It is said that the crowds which came were so immense that by sunrise of the first day there was no space for even one more person. Needless to say, there were no women among the spectators. As Pausanias, the tireless traveller of the second century AD would write: 'On the road to Olympia before you cross the Alpheios river . . . there is a precipitous mountain with high rocks . . . this is

A collapsed column, seen end on, part of the ruins of a Christian basilica on the site of the workshop of Phidias, the sculptor who created much of the Parthenon and the great chryselephantine statue of Zeus at Olympia.

In the fourth century BC, Philip of Macedon erected a pillared rotunda, known as the Philippeion, in his own honor at Olympia.

where the laws of Elis hurl down any woman detected entering the Olympic assembly or even crossing the River Alpheios on the forbidden days.'

According to Pausanias, only one woman ever violated this prohibition. She was Pherenike, whose husband, an Olympic contestant, had died suddenly, leaving his young son to compete in the games in his place. Pherenike accompanied the boy to the games in disguise, so that she could serve as his trainer. When her identity was discovered, she was spared death out of respect for her dead husband, father and brothers, all of whom had been Olympic victors. Some say that it was to prevent any other incident of this sort that trainers thereafter had to enter the precinct naked when they brought their pupils to the games.

Although women could neither compete in nor view the Olympic Games, they had their own festival in the Heraia, held in honor of the goddess Hera, Zeus's wife. The Heraia was also held every four years, but in non-Olympic years. The only events in the Heraia were footraces, evidently because all other athletic contests were considered inappropriate for women. Indeed, although the women contestants raced in the Olympic stadium, they ran a shorter course than did the men in the Olympic footraces. Unlike the male contestants at the Olympic games, the girls and women who competed in the Heraia did not race naked but wore short tunics. Winners did receive olive wreaths, and their victories were celebrated by their home cities, but it was very unusual for a statue of a woman victor to be erected at Olympia.

The Heraia was a distinctly secondary festival compared to the Olympics. By the time the men and boys who were competing arrived at Olympia, they had spent many hours training, and the priests and sanctuary staff had spent at least as many hours readying Olympia for the celebrations. For 10 months before the games, athletes observed strict training and a month before the games took up residence in or near Olympia. There, under the supervision of the Hellenodikai (the

'Judges of the Greeks'), they completed their final training. Nor was this all: while the athletes trained, the Hellenodikai checked to make sure that all were, in fact, Greek, and that there were no imposters among the contestants. In addition, the judges settled controversies over whether a horse should race as a colt or a horse, and whether a contestant should race as a man or a boy. Records were often poorly kept, and questions as to age and nationality were frequent.

Immediately before the festival began, some 48 hours before the opening ceremonies, all the contestants set out for Olympia itself. Gathering spectators as it went, the procession made sacrifices to the immortal gods *en route*. Boasts were made and bets were placed, and the festivities began long before the festival itself.

The games began with a swearing-in ceremony for the athletes at the Council-House which housed the statue of Zeus of the Oaths. Oaths sworn before this statue of Zeus were particularly sacred and binding. The ceremonies concluded with a trumpet fanfare, and then the contests began at the stadium with a competition for trumpet players and heralds. Then the games began in earnest with the boys' running, wrestling and boxing contests.

The running contests were held in Olympia's great stadium, which could seat 40,000 spectators. The stadium's track was 600 Olympic feet; according to one legend, Herakles himself paced off the original track. Although the boys ran naked, the men, who raced on the second day of the five-day games, raced both with and without armor. After the boys' games were completed, the rest of the day was given over to dramatic presentations, recitals and sacrifices.

The second day of the games was taken up with the chariot and horse races, and the most difficult of the Olympic events, the pentathlon. In the pentathlon, the same athlete competes in discus, javelin, jumping, running and wrestling contests. The pentathlon was so demanding that only men competed; boys did not have the necessary strength to go the full course – small wonder if many of the other contestants had the strength of Bubon, the son of Pholos, who threw a stone discus which weighed 316 pounds. Most disci, however, were bronze, lead or marble and weighed between five and 15 pounds.

Jumping, running and wrestling were contests *pour le sport*, but javelin-throwing had a clear practical application: warfare. The javelin, along with the sword, was the standard weapon used by Greek warriors, and skill with a javelin might not only win an olive wreath at Olympia but might save a warrior's life another day. In warfare, the javelin was used by both mounted and foot soldiers, but in the games contests were held only on foot. As with the discus, the winner was the man who threw the javelin furthest; there was no contest between athletes as in Roman gladiatorial games, in which athletes fought hand-to-hand with sword or javelin.

The chariot races at Olympia commemorated Pelops' race for the hand of Hippodameia against Oinomaos – and, because maintaining horses was expensive, the contestants were, like Pelops himself, wealthy aristocrats. Just as there were footraces for men or boys, there were two kinds of horse races, one for colts and the other for full-grown horses. Both horses and colts, however, raced the same courses, which ranged from $2\frac{1}{2}$ to 8 miles. The chariot races were for teams of two or four horses, with both kinds of chariots modeled on the heavier war chariots. In the races, the lighter the chariot, the faster the horses could go – but also the greater the danger to the charioteer, who was bounced around on the rough terrain as he tried to maintain his footing in the wood-and-wickerwork vehicle. The calm figure of the Charioteer of Delphi shows the ideal, not a contestant in mid-race.

The Temple of Hera at Olympia was built circa 700 BC. It is one of the earliest Doric temples still extant. There were two earlier temples on the same site.

Chariots were entered either by wealthy individuals or, in some instances, by entire communities. The charioteer was almost invariably a professional, who drove for pay; the honor of the victory, and the olive crown, went not to the charioteer but to the owner. The flamboyant Athenian politician Alcibiades once entered seven chariots in the Olympic Games, and won prizes in four of the events. Some of those whom Alcibiades defeated alleged that he had stolen and used their horses, a charge which the young Athenian laughed off.

In addition to the chariot races, there were horse races with jockeys riding bareback and without stirrups. Again, most of the jockeys were professionals, although some of the young aristocrats who owned and entered steeds rode them themselves. As with the javelin events, the chariot and horseback events paralleled the martial arts, and cities which won in these events were sending a clear message of military might to their neighbors.

The fourth day of the Olympic Games was given over to wrestling, boxing and the *pankration*, a sufficiently vicious event that most contestants were professionals. Only gouging and biting were forbidden, and the same Alcibiades who was accused of stealing horses for the chariot race was once accused of biting an opponent. As Plutarch tells

Above: The Statue of Hermes by Praxiteles, mentioned by Pausanias, was found in 1877 buried under a pile of rubble. It is one of the few surviving works by that master sculptor.
Right: The Gymnasium at Olympia. The ancient Olympic Games included jumping, throwing the discus, hurling a javelin, wrestling and running.

the story, Alcibiades' opponent shrieked out, 'You bite like a woman, Alcibiades,' to which Alcibiades replied calmly, 'No, like a lion.'

Strangle holds, finger-breaking, stomach kicks and other devious and brutal tactics were employed in the *pankration*, which always drew huge crowds. One victor, Polydamas, was so strong that he strangled a lion with his bare hands, an event commemorated on the base of his victory statue.

Although the athletic events at Olympia went on in the sports complex, which included the stadium, *palaistra*, swimming pool, hippodrome and bath houses, the greater part of Olympia was given over to the religious sanctuary, known as the Altis or 'grove.' Here, on the paths between the great temples to Zeus and Hera, near the altars to Zeus and the other deities, were the statues of the Olympic victors. Here, too, were the treasuries, like those at Delphi, small temple-like structures housing dedications from various city states. In addition to the religious buildings in the Altis, there were civic structures (a council house, various community centers) and an elegant hotel for visitors, the Leonidaion. Visitors who found rooms at the Leonidaion were fortunate indeed; most had to sleep rough, in the meadows around the sanctuary.

From anywhere in the sanctuary, visitors felt the presence of the monumental Temple of Zeus, with its 34 multicolored columns. Inside was the colossal gold-and-ivory statue of Zeus, made by the famous sculptor Pheidias, whose workshop was nearby. The statue, more than 13 meters tall, was so enormous that the Greeks joked that, if Zeus stood up, his head would literally raise the temple roof to the sky. Philo of Byzantium claimed that so much ivory had been used for the statue that elephants must have been created for the express purpose of providing ivory for the Zeus. The statue was one of the Seven Wonders of the World, and visitors were allowed in to see it only on special occasions. Usually only the temple priests were permitted into the innermost recesses of the temple where the Pheidian Zeus sat, its gold and jewels glowing in the darkness.

Near the Temple of Zeus was the smaller temple of Zeus's consort Hera, where the female contestants worshipped. This was the oldest temple at Olympia and, by the fifth century BC, no two of its 34 columns were alike. The original temple had been built with wooden columns and, as each rotted, it had been replaced. With some columns in one style, some in another, the result was a highly idiosyncratic building. One of the many statues in the Temple of Hera was the Hermes of Praxiteles, showing Hermes holding the chubby infant Dionysus.

Not all visitors would have dared, or been permitted, to enter the temples of Zeus and Hera, but all saw the great altar of Zeus which dominated the sanctuary. By the time that Pausanias visited Olympia in the second century AD, the altar stood more than 7 meters high, formed of layer upon layer of ashes from the animals sacrificed here. On one day alone, the Elians, in whose territory Olympia was, sacrificed 100 oxen on this spot. As Pausanias recorded, 'every year . . . the prophets bring the ash from the council house, puddle it with Alpheios water and plaster the altar with it.' In this way, the great altar grew to its imposing height.

Indeed, Pausanias, who travelled the length and breadth of Greece, and marvelled at the Parthenon in Athens and the temple of Apollo at Delphi, awarded the victor's crown to Olympia itself: 'There are a lot of truly wonderful things you can see and hear about in Greece,' he wrote, 'but there is a unique divinity and disposition about the mysteries at Eleusis and the games at Olympia.' In a fragmented world of small city states, great pan-Hellenic sanctuaries such as Delphi and Olympia reminded the Greeks of their common heritage and destiny.

Right: Reconstruction of the East Front of the Temple of Zeus at Olympia, built in the fifth century BC. The sculpture in the pediment shows the start of the race between Pelops and Oinomaos. The figure of Zeus is between them.
Far right: The West front. The pediment sculpture shows the Battle between the Lapiths and the Centaurs, with Apollo in the center.
Below: The Temple of Zeus today. The columns and *stylobate* were built of coarse local limestone.

4. Athens : The School of Greece

Above: The head of the equestrian statue known as the 'Rampin horseman' after the Frenchman who once owned it. The tight curls and archaic smile are typical of sixth-century art. The statue may have been a votive offering.
Left: A marble head of the goddess Hera from the sanctuary near Argos.

Preceding pages: The Temple of Athena Parthenos, or the Parthenon, was the center of the Acropolis of Athens, rebuilt in the fifth century BC, after the Persian Wars.

If the great sanctuaries such as Delphi and Olympia are thought of as providing integrating forces for the Greeks of these centuries, there were undeniably opposing forces at work. Of all the rival city-states responsible for the latter, Athens deserves the most credit for thriving on the tension of these conflicting forces – and blame for contributing to the tension. This side of Athens is often avoided or overlooked by those who prefer to concentrate on the great architecture, handsome sculpture or beautiful vase-paintings of 'the golden age of Athens,' but it was never overlooked by those contemporaries who often found themselves abused by the 'golden Athenians.' When Pericles boasted that Athens was 'the school of the Greeks,' there would have been some bitterly ironic support for this from many reluctant students.

How did this come about? Athens, as we have already seen, was by no means the leader of the Greek people during their early centuries. Even with the great awakening at the end of the 'Dark Age,' Athens was overshadowed both culturally and commercially by several more progressive city-states – not only those in Ionia, along the coast of Asia Minor, but even by neighbors such as Corinth. Yet the Athenians somehow managed to retain a sense of themselves as special, even superior people. Their great historian Thucydides would write: 'Attica, since time immemorial, has been inhabited by the same race of people.' Whether true or not, or whether truer than for other Greek city-states, the Athenians seemed to draw upon this sense of themselves. The city had indeed been a Mycenaean center, but hardly of the first rank, while its evident insulation from the ravages that accompanied the coming of the Dorians allowed the Athenians to regard themselves as somehow 'purer' than many of their neighbors. Yet despite Athens' pre-eminence in fields such as sculpture and vase painting by the sixth century, it was still not that far ahead of other city-states. When it came to temples, for instance, Corfu, Olympia, Delphi and Corinth – why, even provincial colonies such as Selinus and Paestum in Sicily and Italy – could all claim superior examples. Wherein, then lay Athens' strength?

Probably such a question can never be answered, but one factor must have been the area where Athens did seem to demonstrate precocious development – its government. Even there, although Athens had abolished its hereditary monarchy relatively early – by 683 BC – it was still an élite group of adult males who elected the nine *archons*, the chief rulers, and aristocratic families continued to hold onto as much power as they could. And when Athens elected Draco as a special commissioner to codify the laws and alleviate the continuing tensions between rich and poor, his severe reforms still favored the wealthy landowners. The use of money from about 650 BC onwards was forcing small landowners and urban poor deeper into debt, and by 594 BC the situation in Attica-Athens was so explosive that the Athenian citizens – still that small group of upper-class men – elected an *archon* to whom they gave unprecedented legislative power to effect more fundamental reforms.

This was Solon – an aristocrat but not wealthy, a poet and man of broad culture, and above all a man able to assert power without seizing it. He moved quickly to introduce what were actually quite radical changes for that day: he restored freedom or land to many who had lost one or both while indebted; converted the monetary system of Athens from the standard of Aegina to that of Corinth, a more dynamic and international market economy; granted citizenship to craftsmen and tradesmen who settled in Athens; and encouraged the cultivation of olives while prohibiting the export of cereal grains. Most far-reaching of all, he divided citizens into four classes – and although land remained the basis of citizenship, the amount required was quite modest; beyond

Left: A covered *amphora*, decorated with a black-figure painting of a wedding procession by the Athenian master painter Exekias, *c* 540 BC).
Right: The front seats of the Theater of Dionysus were reserved for the chief priest and the city elders.
Bottom: The Theater of Dionysus was remodeled in Roman times, but the uppermost seats may date back to the fifth century BC.
Below: Decorative detail of a water course in the Theater of Dionysus in Athens.

that, citizens of all four classes could now belong to the assembly, or *ecclesia*, which gave them the right to elect officials, vote on laws and generally determine issues of war and peace.

Yet for all these relatively radical reforms, the government of Athens was still far from a genuine democracy, the upper classes – the old wealthy landowners – continuing to hold most of the power. Meanwhile, the old-guard conservatives were unhappy about the enfranchisement of any new groups. Solon himself went into voluntary exile after introducing his reforms, and tensions immediately flared up, especially between the two extremes – the landed aristocracy and those who made their money from the crafts or commerce. Out of this emerged a leader of a third force, Pisastratus, a hero of Athens' conflict with nearby Megara; by 560 BC, after two failed attempts, he had installed himself as the tyrant of Athens.

Like all tyrants of this era, Pisastratus knew how to appeal to the masses: he expropriated land from some enemies and distributed it among the peasantry, he loaned farmers money from his own mines and remained accessible to anyone with a complaint. But he did not really share any power, and he kept his own mercenary private army while holding the Acropolis as a private citadel. But Pisastratus also introduced a number of progressive reforms: he coined new silver money – with the sacred owl of the Acropolis on one side and the goddess Athena on the other – that at once became the reserve currency of international trade in the Mediterranean; he supported new projects such as developing a city water supply; and he encouraged the arts so that, for instance, Athenian red-figure vases soon displaced Corinthian and other vases as the most prized works; and he promoted the rebirth of the old Homeric religion by introducing elements from the Homeric epics into the Panathenaean festival that celebrated the unification of Attica.

Two of Pisastratus's undertakings were to leave particular imprints on the future city of Athens. He constructed a temple to Olympian Zeus in a sanctuary dedicated to that deity just outside the city walls, southwest of the Acropolis. It would be replaced by a colossal temple begun by his sons, Hipparchus and Hippias, but they only succeeded in

Above left: Obverse of an Athenian ten drachma coin, struck in 486 BC, bearing the head of the goddess.
Above right: Reverse of an Athenian ten drachma coin bearing the symbol of an owl.
Below: The Temple of Zeus was built in the elaborate Corinthian style.

Above: The Temple of Olympian Zeus, first planned in the fifth century BC, was completed by the Emperor Hadrian.

getting the *stylobate*, or great base, laid down before the former was killed and the latter expelled. The colossal *stylobate* would sit there for over three centuries until building recommenced about 174 BC; then it was not until about AD 130 and under the Roman Emperor Hadrian that the largest temple in mainland Greece was completed.

The other major legacy to Athenians from Pisastratus was his promulgation of the cult of Dionysus, the god of wine and fertility. He organized a new festival, the Great Dionysia of the City. One of its main attractions was a 'goat song' sung by a choir of Dionysus' attendants dressed in goatskins; this eventually evolved into the recitation of a story; then two or more choirs began to compete to sing the best story in a so-called 'tragic' contest. With the addition of actors to dramatize the stories, the contests eventually assumed the form of Greek drama that would remain one of the highest peaks of human culture. A circular orchestra, or dancing ground, was set aside for these events on the base of the Acropolis in the sixth century; by the early fifth century, wooden stands were erected for spectators; an earthen auditorium was formed sometime in the first quarter of the fifth century; and by about 330 BC the stone theater that later generations would know as the Theater of Dionysus was erected.

But if the Temple of Olympian Zeus and the Theater of Dionysus were Pisastratus' memorials in a distant future, his more immediate legacy to his fellow Athenians was a period of political turmoil. His sons, Hipparchus and Hippias, assumed power at his death, but Hipparchus

Above: One of the masterpieces of fifth-century sculpture, the bronze Poseidon was found in the water off Cape Artemisium. The inlaid eyes and the trident have disappeared.

Right: Relief sculpture from a grave at Eleusis. The drapery and musculature are typical of the late fifth century BC.
Far right: A sixth-century bronze of Apollo. The archaic smile and patterned hair are characteristic.

was assassinated in 514 BC by Aristogiton and Harmodius, and in 510 BC Hippias was forced into exile by a combination of disaffected Athenians and Spartans. Now a new aristocratic Athenian family, the Alcmaeonids, began to assert power and one of their number, Cleisthenes, introduced yet another series of reforms that extended democracy a bit further. It was far from a popular democracy as later eras would understand the concept: women, slaves and resident aliens were still denied citizenship, and the old landed and monied aristocracy still tended to hold the higher offices. But by about 500 BC, it could be said that Athenians had gone farther than any other people in the world at that time to involve large numbers of citizens in the governing process.

And now for the first time the city-state of Athens – and probably all of the Greek city-states – was to be challenged by a foreign power: the Persian Empire. It was typical of the Athenian spirit, for better or worse, that the conflict with Persia was not one that Athens necessarily had to undertake. Since 547 BC, the Ionian-Greek city-states along the coast of Asia Minor had been under the rule of the Persians, the most powerful empire of that time. On the one hand, the Persians ruled with a

Left: Above the columns of the Parthenon, the metopes and triglyphs can be seen. The frieze beyond them shows the procession for the Panathenaic Festival.
Right: The bronze ligatures that bound the base of the Parthenon together have been removed, but the openings cut for them are still visible.
Below: The metopes of the Parthenon were reliefs illustrating famous combats between the Centaurs and Lapiths, or Gods and Giants.

relatively light hand, allowing the Ionian Greeks to keep their own language, religion and customs. But the Ionians had to pay taxes and tribute to their Persian overlords, and were essentially powerless within the Persian state system. By 499 BC, some of these Ionian city-states revolted against the Persians and immediately appealed for support from Greek city-states on the mainland.

Athens and Eritria, a city-state on Euboea, sent ships to aid the Ionians – Sparta, typically, refused to become involved in such an enterprise – but by 493 the revolt was crushed. That might have been the end of the conflict had Darius I, the Persian Emperor, not decided that Athens had to be taught a lesson: perhaps not unjustifiably, he suspected that the Athenians were not going to rest content with their present commercial or territorial ambitions. Darius mounted an expedition in 492 BC, but after taking Thrace, Macedonia and the island of Thasos, the Persians were forced to return home by a storm. But in the summer of 490 BC, Darius sent a fleet across the Aegean, this time determined to strike directly at the heartland of the Greeks. The showdown came on the plain of Marathon, some 26 miles north of Athens, where some 10,000 Athenian troops confronted about twice that many

Persian troops. Although outnumbered, the Athenians had the advantage of knowing the terrain, and they tricked the Persians into breaking through the thin center force on the plain and then swept down from the slopes on the wings to force the Persians into a disorganized retreat to their ships. When they sailed away, the Persians left behind seven ships and 6400 dead: the Athenians had lost only 192.

But it was by no means the last confrontation between the Persians and the Greeks: in fact, these two peoples would continue their hostilities for over two centuries. The most immediate result, however, was that Persia set about to avenge the defeat at Marathon. By 480 BC, the Persians had sent an army estimated at 180,000 men around the Aegean and into northern Greece, where they were joined by a fleet of 700 ships. But the Greeks had not remained idle during this decade, either. Led by Themistocles, Athens had invested vast sums in a war fleet – the 'wooden wall' that the oracle of Delphi had said was the only hope against the Persians. Themistocles had also formed an alliance with Sparta and other Greek city-states and had even allowed Sparta to head this Greek League. It is tempting to attribute this to Athenian cleverness – letting Sparta take the blame if the Persians triumphed, but letting Athens take credit for stepping aside if the Persians were defeated.

In the end, the Persians did both, and Sparta was indeed the loser. The Greeks' strategy was to allow the Persians to move southward and inflict gradual losses on their increasingly isolated forces. At the narrow pass at Thermopylae, the Persians overwhelmed the reduced forces led by Leonidas, the Spartan general, and all his troops except two were killed. As the Persians advanced on Athens, the Athenians abandoned their city – again, part of their strategic gamble; the Persians moved in and sacked or burned most of the buildings, including those on the Acropolis. But on 23 September 480 BC, the Greeks took their revenge when their fleet outmaneuvered the Persians in the Bay of Salamis, west of the Athenians' port of Piraeus; as the Emperor Xerxes sat on a throne above the bay, about 200 of the Persian ships were destroyed and the remaining hundreds fled out to sea. It was the next year, 479 BC, that the Persians were conclusively defeated – on land at Plataea in central Greece, and at sea at Mycale near Miletus on the coast of Asia Minor – and the Greeks seemed at least temporarily free of the Persian menace when they decisively defeated them at the Eurymedon River in Asia Minor in 467 BC.

Meanwhile, another threat had emerged among the Greeks: Athens. Not only had they quickly set about to rebuild a religious and ceremonial center worthy of their aspirations out of the ashes of their Acropolis, Athens also set out to establish a political organization that would provide a unified front against foreign threats such as the Persians from the disarray of the Greek city-states. Formed in 478 BC, the alliance was known as the Delian League, after the island of Delos, long a sacred site to many Greeks and now the location of the league's treasury and assembly. But from the outset, it was clear that Athens was the true center of power. All members of the league were bound by individual treaties to Athens, and all members accepted that Athens would have as much power as all of them combined. But the Delian League was more than just treaties: members contributed either a designated number of fully-equipped warships or assigned sums of money. And it was not long before Athens began to force members to contribute money to build ships in the Athenians' shipyards, assigning its own sailors to man these ships. As Athens became more and more assertive, it forced other city-states to stay in the League and imposed its own rule over those city-states that resisted Athenian policy. Then in 454 BC, Athens eliminated even the façade of what had become a hollow

Left : Riders in the Panathenaic Procession from the Parthenon frieze. The figures are idealized.

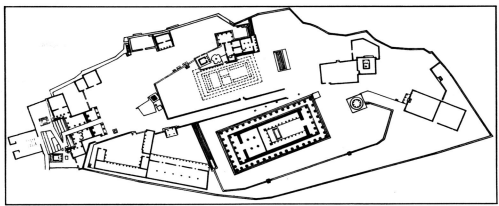

Left: The Acropolis, Athens. Below the
Parthenon is the Theater of Herodes.
Top: Plan of the Acropolis: The
Propylaea or Gateway is on the far left.
Above the Parthenon are the
foundations of an earlier temple. The
round temple on the right was dedicated
to Rome and Augustus.
Above: Athena flying her owl: a fifth-
century BC statuette.

league by transferring the actual treasury from Delos to the Acropolis. With the subsequent elimination of any assemblies on Delos and the imposition of Athenian currency on all the league's city-states, Athens was now effectively running an empire.

By this time, too, another crucial force had emerged on the Greek scene: Athens had a man who, although not truly the sole ruler, was to be the dominant personality for a quarter-century. This was Pericles, a descendant of the Alcmaeonids who had long been prominent in Athens. A reserved, even haughty man, Pericles did not pretend to be a man of the people, but he held the respect of most Athenians because of his incorruptible behavior, his commitment to the ideals of Athens' form of constitutional democracy and his generally intelligent policies. His base of power was the office of *strategos*, the commanding general, a position he held first about 453 BC and then throughout most of the years until his death in 429 BC, yet it was his administration of the city of Athens that would mark his rule as 'the golden age' of ancient Greece.

The first few years of Pericles' predominance in Athens' public life were not distinguished by any major architectural changes on the Acropolis itself; rather, he seems to have initiated the construction of the Long Walls that connected Athens to its port, Piraeus. But when some 8000 talents from the treasury of the Delian League were deposited on the Acropolis in 454 BC, Pericles saw the chance to make Athens a true religious and artistic beacon for all Greeks. To give some idea of just how much 8000 talents was worth, a trireme – the finest three-bank oared ship of the Athenian navy – cost only three talents: the Parthenon, Propylaea and several other buildings on the Acropolis would cost some 2012 talents, while the statue of Athena that stood within the Parthenon would alone cost some 700 talents.

To direct the construction of the new buildings on the Acropolis, Pericles called upon a friend, Phidias the sculptor. Phidias called upon many architects and sculptors to do the work – in particular, the architects Iktinus and Kallikrates – but it was Pericles and Phidias who provided the co-ordination and conception of the whole that assured a stylistic unity. The first building actually commissioned was a small Temple of Athena Nike ('Athena as Victory', although the temple would often incorrectly be called Nike Apteros, or 'Wingless Victory'). This

Top left: The Parthenon is recognizable by the eight columns at each end, and the 17 along each side. Those at the corners are thicker than the rest, but an optical illusion makes them appear to be the same size.

Above: The Temple of Nike (Victory) near the Propylaea is built in the Ionic style.

was commissioned in 449 BC to celebrate the just-signed Treaty of Callias, a peace treaty with Persia; the architect Kallikrates designed it, but for reasons not entirely known its actual construction was delayed until 427–424 BC. The bastion on which it stands had originally been part of the Mycenaean fortress, and an altar and sanctuary dedicated to Athena Nike had been erected here in the sixth century BC, but it was destroyed by the Persians in 480 BC.

The first new building actually begun was the Parthenon in 447 BC, but it was erected on the site of a temple that had been started in 488 BC; a massive limestone substructure had been embedded into the natural stone of the Acropolis, the marble *stylobate* had been placed over this, and the first column drums had been put in place before the Persians burned it in 480 BC. Iktinus and Kallikrates, charged with building this new Parthenon, changed the proportions of the temple (making it somewhat shorter but wider than the previous one), but they were able to

Left: Within the colonnade of the Parthenon can be seen the ruins of the *cella*, where the great statue of Athena by Phidias stood.

Below: A late sixth-century red-figure *kylix*, by the master potter Euxitheos and the master painter Euphronios, showing the death of Sarpedon during the Trojan War.

utilize much of the already cut stone. Although in its general plan the Parthenon was in the line of Doric-style temples – such as the Temple of Apollo at Corinth – it actually deviated from the basic design in almost every detail. The internal arrangement of walls and rooms, the colonnade, the use of Ionic columns – all these were radical departures; meanwhile, such devices as the inward inclination of the corner columns, the slight bulge at the center of the columns and the slight curving of

Below left : The Parthenon and the Acropolis stand high above the city of Athens.

the horizontal lines – all to compensate for the optical illusions resulting from the massive stonework – further reveal the level of sophistication and refinement of the architects of Athens of this time.

By the Great Panathenaic Festival of 438 BC, Phidias's chryselephantine (gold and ivory) statue of Athena Parthenos was dedicated in the *cella*. Standing some 50 feet high, it used about 250 pounds of gold and must have been a work of almost barbaric splendor. Phidias's

reputation in antiquity was based on this work, but aside from the fact that no traces of the statue remain (it is known through smaller versions in carvings and sculptures), most modern peoples have far higher regard for the sculptural decorations of the Parthenon – the pediments, frieze and *metopes*. Their subject-matter was undoubtedly set by Pericles and other leading Athenians, but Phidias designed them and then made models in clay and plaster for sculptors who worked under him. These required the stonecarvers to reproduce effects in marble like subtle folds of drapery and details of musculature previously never tried in stone; the resultant Parthenon sculptures would influence all subsequent Greek sculpture.

Above: The head of a horse from the east pediment of the Parthenon. The rivet holes on the horses' heads indicate that reins and bridles of bronze once adorned the sculptures.

Right: A metope from the Parthenon, now in the British Museum, describes a battle between the Lapiths and the Centaurs.

Right: A metope from the Parthenon, now in the British Museum, describes a battle between the Lapiths and the Centaurs.

Although the Parthenon was dedicated in 438 BC, its sculptures and certain other elements were not completed till 432 BC; in the meantime, work on two other major structures on the Acropolis had commenced. One was the Propylaea, the monumental 'gateway' designed by Mnesicles and constructed between 437–432 BC. There had been earlier gateways to the Acropolis, but they had been aligned somewhat differently and none was so ambitious as this. Although Mnesicles' original design had to be somewhat modified, its proportions were congruent with those of the Parthenon, a fact indicative of the total planning of the Acropolis; its construction was halted by the Peloponnesian War, however, and the Propylaea was never completed.

The other building begun at this time was the Erechtheum, but construction had barely been begun before it too was halted by the Peloponnesian War; evidently almost completed by 408 BC, it was damaged by fire and not completed until 395 BC. Formed of several almost distinct architectural units – one of which, the Erechtheum, has given its name to the whole – this edifice rises at about the midpoint of the northern side of the Acropolis on the site of the palace of the Mycenaean kings and the place where some of the most ancient and sacred traditions of Athens were centered. The name Erechtheum comes from a legendary early king of Athens who at some point became identified with the god of the sea and earthquakes Poseidon; a cult grew up that worshipped the deity on this site.

But the deeper significance of this very site involved various other deities and legends. Here was said to be the tomb of Kekrops, the mythical first king of Athens, and here, too, lived the serpent that had been the early custodian of the rock on this site. Behind all these lay still

Far left: The columns of the south porch of the Erechtheum are caryatids, or maidens.
Left: A grave *stele* on the Acropolis shows a figure wrapped in the Greek mantle or *himation.*
Bottom left: The base of an Ionic column showing the rounded base and the channels on the column shaft.

another myth, telling how Athena and Poseidon had, in the reign of Kekrops, contested for control of Athens and Attica, and here, on this very spot, Athena had made an olive tree grow while Poseidon had struck the rock with his trident and made a spring of salt water gush forth. All these myths, legends and cults were inextricably involved in making the Erechtheum one of the most sacred of all locales in Athens.

Although these works were the major ones on the Acropolis, they were by no means the only structures or sculptures there. In fact, much of the Acropolis was covered with the many walls, gateways, temples, sanctuaries, altars, pedestals, statues and other works, most of them made out of marble or other stone and virtually all painted in a spectrum of colors that must have made the Acropolis a dazzling, if distracting, complex. Add to this the constant fires and smoke emanating from the numerous sacrifices and offerings and the comings and goings of Greeks paying their respects to their gods, and the Acropolis was far removed from later ages' image of ancient Athens as the serene, white-marbled, restrained temple of classicism.

Yet another impressive structure that was erected during the age of Pericles is one that has long been mistakenly known as the Theseion, situated on a low hill at the northwest corner of the Agora. It received this name in the Middle Ages because it was thought to have been a sanctuary built about 475 BC to hold the bones of Theseus, his feats depicted by carvings on the *metopes*; it is now known to be a temple dedicated to Hephaistos and Athena, and so might better be called the Hephaistion. Neither as delicate nor as imposing as its contemporary

Below: The coffered ceilings of ancient Greek buildings were thought to have been pierced to let in the light.

109

the Parthenon, this temple was to survive the centuries in surprisingly good condition, a solid witness to the pervasiveness of Athenians' religious dedication and civic pride.

The Hephaistion, or Theseion, testifies in another way to this double loyalty of the Athenians – for unlike the great monuments of the Acropolis that were literally set on the 'high point of the city' (*akropolis*), this temple was situated close to the hustle and bustle of the everyday life of the city. During its earlier centuries, Athens was concentrated on and around the Acropolis, while numerous small settlements or neighborhoods were scattered on the fringes, each with its own local shrines and marketplaces. But as Athens grew and prospered and as the Acropolis served as a magnet for more and more elaborate religious and ceremonial activities, there also grew up a central *agora* for all of Attica, a place not just as a place to conduct business but as a center of secular/ civic life, for *agora* really means 'assembly.' The original Agora of Athens was probably closer to the western approach to the Acropolis, but by the sixth century BC its current site was being developed: the first Bouleuterion, or Council House, was erected in this area during the time of Solon, early in that century. A great drain that was built through the site during the rule of Kleisthenes, at the end of the sixth century, brought fresh water from the nearby hills and served as a focal point for further development.

Even before that, however, the Agora was becoming associated with the public life of Athens. It was in the Agora, for instance, that Hipparchus, the son of Pisastratus, was assassinated in 514 BC by Aristogiton and Harmodius. Although their motives were more personal than political, they were soon being regarded as pioneers of democratic idealism, and a statue of these 'tyrannicides' was erected in the Agora

Above: Each metope on the entablature was separated by a triglyph. These were the beam ends in wooden temples and remained as a stylized element in later marble ones.

Previous pages: The Propylaea, or great gate, of the Acropolis. Beside it at an angle is the small temple of Nike Apteros.

by about 505 BC; this was carried off by the Persians in their sack of 480 BC, but a new version was made by Kritias and Nesiotes. (Alexander the Great would later bring the original group back from Persepolis, but eventually both versions were destroyed.)

Elsewhere in the Agora are other sites and structures that would resonate through the ages. There was the Tholos, or Prytanikon, where the 50 governing *prytanes* of the day would gather to dine (at public expense) and discuss the agenda for the state's affairs. There was the Stoa Poikile, 'the painted portico,' so named because it had plaques (probably wooden) painted by the leading painters of the fifth century and depicting scenes from famous battles such as Troy and Marathon; it was in this *stoa* that Zeno the philosopher taught in the third century BC and thus his school became known as 'the Stoics.' (Centuries later, another provocative man, Paul of Tarsus, would appear in the Agora and argue about his new faith in Christ.)

Even more than the Acropolis, the Agora was crowded with structures of all kinds – countless statues on pedestals, government buildings, altars, small temples and *stoas*, porticos in which people took refuge from the hot sun or cold while they discussed affairs. But the Agora was also the locale of the city's commercial life – where merchants made arrangements for the buying and selling of goods, where money was exchanged, where importers and exporters struck deals that affected trade throughout the Mediterranean world. And since it was largely a man's world, here in the Agora were the barbershops. There was even a cobbler's shop, that of Simon, where Socrates was said to have held forth when he wasn't over at the Stoa of Zeus Eleutherios – for Socrates chose to be a 'gadfly' not only in respect to accepted ideas but also of the conventional behavior of philosophers.

Far left: Within the Doric colonnade of the fifth-century temple sacred to Hephaistos.
Left: The metopes of the Hephaistion show episodes in the lives of Theseus and Herakles.
Below: The Hephaistion stands on a hill above the Agora, which was the civic and commercial center of Athens.

Above: Remains of the cult statue of Apollo Patroos by Euphranor, show the sense of balance in the figure as well as a delight in the pattern created by the fall of fabric.
Left: Fragment of a statue of Themis (Divine Justice), which once stood before the Royal Stoa.
Top right: Monumental base celebrating victory in a chariot race. Such dedications might be made at the time of the event or upon the death of the victor.
Right: Relief commemorating a victory in an equestrian event. The riders seem to be individual portraits.

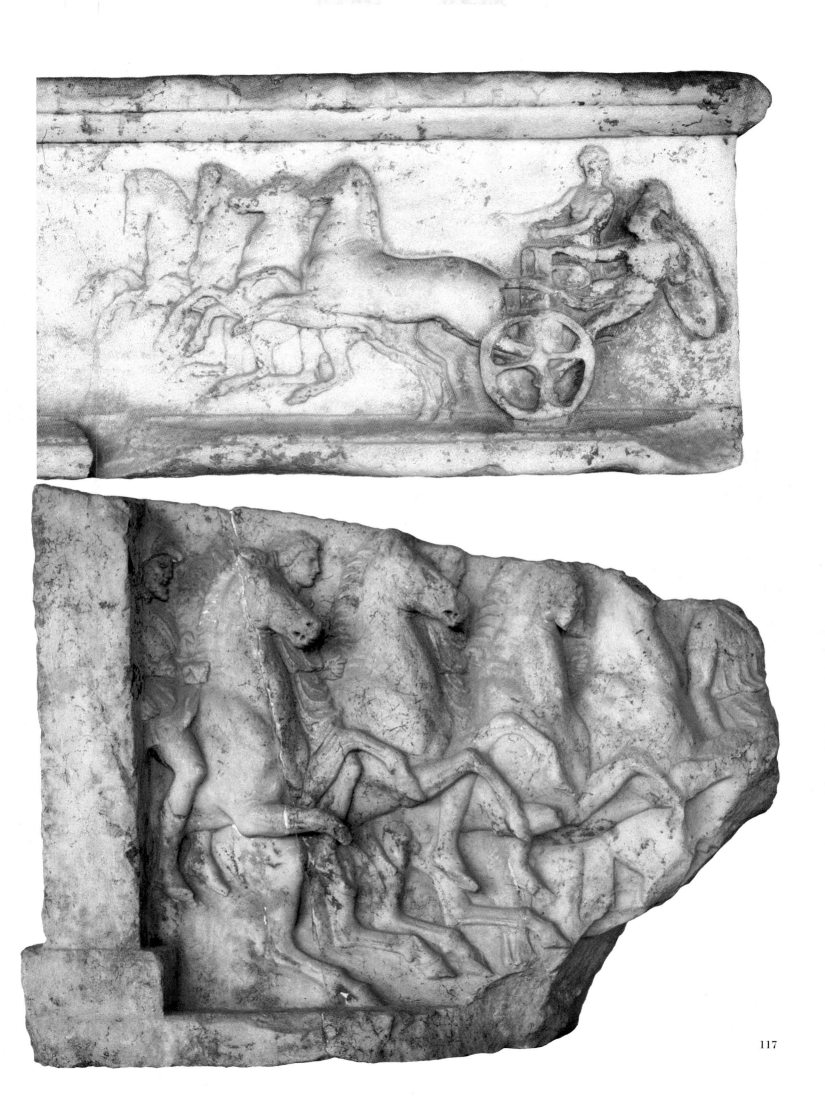

Above: Statue of the Roman Emperor Hadrian, who built part of the city wall and completed the Temple of Olympian Zeus.

Above left: A statue within the Odeion of Agrippa, the first covered theater built in 15 BC during the Roman Occupation.

Left: Beneath the Agora ran a covered drainage system.

Top right: The Agora was surrounded by small shops and houses whose ruins are now uncovered.

Right: On the west side of the Agora, below the Hephaistion, are the ruins of the Council House and several temples.

Socrates also serves as a reminder that the glory and fame of Athens did not depend entirely upon its great architecture, its sculptures or even its commercial and civic affairs. Much of its 'treasure' lay in less tangible achievements. For several centuries, Athens both nurtured and attracted a succession of illustrious dramatists, poets, historians, philosophers, orators and 'wordsmiths': Aeschylus, Sophocles, Euripides and Aristophanes all had their plays produced in the theater at the foot of the Acropolis. Herodotus, Thucydides and Xenophon recorded the immediate past and present of the Greeks in works that would be studied by future civilizations. Lysias, Isocrates and Demosthenes were only some of the better-known orators whose stirring words reverberated through ancient Athens and across the ages. Indeed, the philosophers who were active in Athens during these years – Parmenides, Zeno, Gorgias, Protagoras, Socrates, Plato and Aristotle – themselves constituted a national treasure that any civilization would be proud to claim.

To this extent, then, Athens was indeed 'the school of the Greeks' in the best and most idealistic sense. But there was that other sense, the institutions and discipline imposed – often harshly – on the powerless. Women, as has been noted, had no voice in public life and most had no property or other rights; in fact, they had virtually no role to play outside the home, although in practice many probably exercised considerable influence from this 'power base.' There were the slaves – a most conservative estimate assigns some 60,000 to Athens alone by the end of the fifth century BC – who, whether they were doing the hardest work in the silver mines or relatively mild work in domestic service, were effectively treated as property, not as human beings. And even a Pericles, the finest flower of Athenian manhood, could be ruthless when it came to those who stood in Athens' way. Once the island of Samos ignored some orders from Athens, so Pericles himself set off across the Aegean, imposed a new government on Samos, fined the islanders and then imprisoned hostages before returning to Athens. When Samians revolted Pericles immediately sailed back and, after a nine-month siege, recaptured the island; he forced the Samians to destroy their walls and their fleet and imposed another government totally subservient to the autocratic rule of Athens.

Above: The view from the Hephaistion east to the Acropolis. *Above left:* Egg and dart molding combined with bead and reel on a marble fragment of the Acropolis.

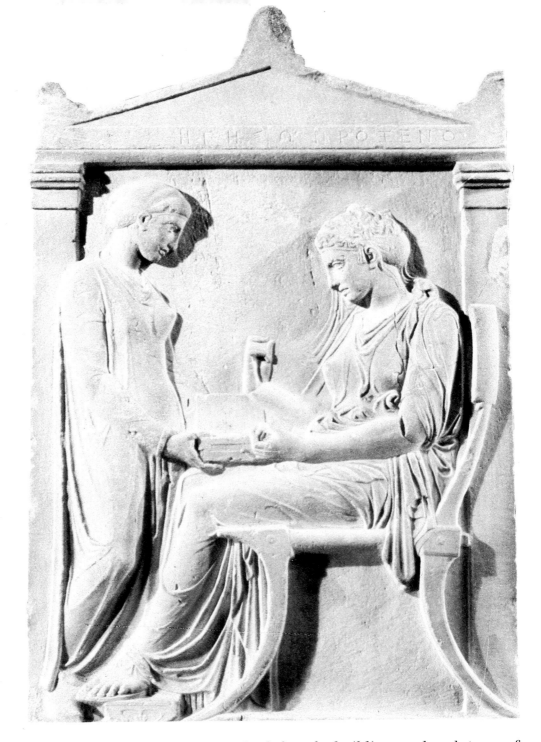

Above right: The fifth-century grave *stele* of a woman named Hegeso choosing a necklace from the jewel box held by her maid.
Following pages: The view across the Agora at sunset.

So, just as it must be recognized that the buildings and sculptures of Athens were not left as pure white marble; just as it must be recognized that the Athenians moved constantly, and unconsciously, between their religious shrines and their commercial affairs; and just as it must be recognized that the 'golden years' of the Athenians were not without their dark shadows, so it must be recognized that Athens and its people did not live in some remote and ideal society, surrounded by tasteful works of art and isolated from the passions and tensions of their age. The people of Athens, at least the middle and upper classes, were an inquisitive, dynamic people, constantly moving back and forth between the settled 'knowns' of their own city and the stimulating 'unknowns' of the world outside Athens. Whether it was to participate in some secret rite at Eleusis or take the cure at a health resort like Epidauros, to make a pilgrimage to the home of their Ionian heritage at Delos or to visit some remote natural locale to be closer to their gods at Sounion or Bassae, Athenians joined their fellow Greeks in celebrating their place in the world at large.

Below: A fifth-century bronze mirror has a handle in the shape of the goddess Aphrodite.

Bottom: Shoulder piece of a bronze cuirass, *c* 400 BC, bears a decorative relief of a warrior battling an Amazon.

124

Right: Bronze mirror cover, fourth century BC, with a decorative etching of Aphrodite attended by a small winged cupid gaming with the goat-footed god Pan.
Bottom: Bronze gryphon head of the seventh century BC, thought to have been part of a tripod.
Below: Bronze ram from the Greek colony at Syracuse on Sicily.

Below: Mounted figure of a warrior from a Greek colony in Southern Italy.

Above: Painting on the inside of a *kylix* or drinking cup from the workshops of Euphronios (*c* 500 BC). Genre scenes like this peasant boy on horseback were popular.

Above: Vase painting by the Dikalos painter, *c* 500 BC, of Athenian youths and their *hetairai* (girlfriends).
Top left: Black-figure *lekythos*, or oil jar, with a painting of Poseidon on a winged seahorse (early fifth century BC).
Top right: Protocorinthian cinerary *amphora* from Athens, *c* 1000 BC.
Left: Corinthian wine jug from about 600 BC. The fantastic beasts were part of a Near Eastern influence.
Right: Jar with red-figure painting of a youth carrying a couch and table, *c* 180 BC. Much of Greek daily life is known from the glimpses available on pottery.

Left: The so-called '*Peplos kore*,' from the style of her dress, which bears traces of the original paint. Her archaic smile and stylized hair were also highly colored.
Below: Hellenistic sculpture of Ajax, the Greek hero, holding the wounded Patroclus during the Trojan War.

Right: A sixth-century *kouros* known as the 'Apollo of Terrea.' It is a more primitive work than the contemporary *kore*.

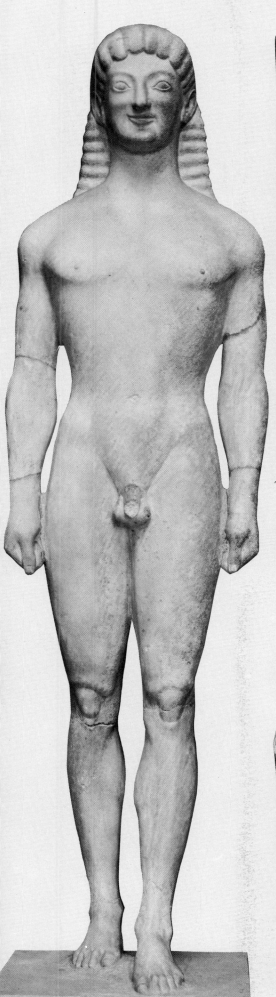

Above: A metope from the Parthenon: a Centaur overpowering a Lapith. All the Parthenon sculptures are thought to have been planned in the workshops of Phidias.

Below: The gods Poseidon, Apollo and Artemis seated at the Panathenaic Procession, from the Parthenon frieze.

5. The Sacred Sites

Every Greek household had a family altar, each city had numerous shrines, private religious societies had their own ceremonies, and all the Greeks worshipped at the pan-Hellenic sanctuaries such as Delphi and Olympia. Although Delphi and Olympia were the most important of the sacred sites in Greece, they were by no means the only important ones. There were sacred sites such as Sounion and Bassae, temples which stood in splendid isolation and were visited primarily by locals. There were also sites such as Eleusis, Epidauros and Delos which drew visitors from throughout the Greek world. And, while Epidauros and Delos were open to all visitors, Eleusis reserved much of its sanctuary for initiates in the Eleusinian Mysteries.

The Greeks had no priestly caste; any individual could serve as priest or prophet. Often powerful families had a monopoly on a local priesthood, as at the great sanctuary of Eleusis. Often, too, young women or men would serve the gods for a number of years and then return to normal life, their priestly service behind them. The Greeks were polytheists, and they had, therefore, a wide range of religious rites, rituals and sacred sites. Saint Paul would call the Greeks 'very God-fearing,' a polite way of saying that they were superstitious, with too many gods and too many shrines. Yet the sacred sites of Greece were important to all Greeks, and of these sites Eleusis, Epidauros, Delos, Sounion and Bassae were among the most revered.

ELEUSIS

Eleusis was the site of the Eleusinian Mysteries, rites so secret that no initiate ever fully divulged the nature of the ceremonies. As Pausanias, who had been initiated in the Mysteries, wrote: 'The dream forbids me to write what lies inside the sanctuary wall, and what the uninitiate are not allowed to see they obviously ought not to know about.'

What *is* known, however, is that the rites at Eleusis concerned the goddess Demeter, whose own daughter Persephone had been abducted by Hades, god of the Underworld. Demeter, frantic, wandered across the entire Greek world searching for her child until, exhausted, she sat down to rest on a smooth rock beside a refreshing spring at Eleusis. There she was sitting when a group of Eleusinian maidens found her.

The maidens took Demeter with them to the palace of the King of Eleusis, where she spent the next year. In her terrible grief over Persephone Demeter laid a curse on the land, and no crops grew anywhere in Greece. This was particularly hard on the Eleusinians, whose livelihood depended on their rich grain fields. Finally, the King of the Gods, Zeus himself, took pity on the starving mortals and sent his messenger, Hermes, to look for Persephone. Hermes found Persephone in the palace of Hades, king of the underworld. Hades at first refused to release Persephone, whom he had made his wife, but ultimately relented and allowed her to spend half the year with her mother. The other six months Persephone was doomed to spend in the underworld with Hades in punishment for breaking her fast and eating six pomegranate seeds.

Demeter was so delighted to receive her daughter back from the underworld for even half the year that she gave the young Eleusinian prince Triptolemos the gift of grain and knowledge of the secrets of cultivation. Bounty returned to the earth, and the Eleusinians honored Demeter by building her a great shrine.

This is how the Greeks explained the origins of the Eleusinian Mysteries and, as their wise men knew, the myth of Demeter and Persephone explained the harvest cycle in which the earth lies bare for half the

Above: An early Attic amphora in the Geometric style found at Eleusis.
Top right: Remains of the Propylaea at Eleusis, site of the secret rites known as the Eleusinian Mysteries, which celebrated the cycle of death and rebirth in nature.
Right: A wellhead at Eleusis, almost intact.

132

Above: Demeter's Cave at Eleusis, sacred to the goddess of grain, who was worshipped seasonally by the common people.

Right: A marble relief from about 440 BC, showing Demeter on the left and her daughter Persephone on the right, turned inward toward the boy Triptolemos, who is being sent out to teach agriculture to the world.

Top far left: A Greek sphinx ornaments a Roman sarcophagus at Eleusis.

Left: The Hall of Mysteries at Eleusis was part of the great building program undertaken by Pericles in the fifth century BC, which included the Parthenon.

year and is fruitful for the other half. In addition to explaining this annual cycle of growth, the Eleusinian Mysteries presumably addressed the yet greater mystery of death and rebirth through an afterlife. Whereas most Greek religious observances were familial or civic, Eleusis held out hope for the individual of a life beyond – and better than – the present.

For this reason, the Eleusinian Mysteries appealed to Greeks of all walks of life, and were open to freeman and slave alike. Indeed, as time went on, the Mysteries were open to non-Greeks as well as to Greeks. As the 'Hymn to Demeter' celebrated, 'Happy is he among the men that populate the earth who saw these things, because he who was *not* initiated into the Mysteries and did not take part in them will not share the same happy fate when he dies and is in wretched darkness.'

The sanctuary of Eleusis was only 22 miles from Athens, in the district of Attica, which Athens controlled. First the Eleusinians themselves and then their more powerful neighbors, the Athenians, controlled the sanctuary at Eleusis. Many of the monuments at the site were believed to have been there since the visit of Demeter. There was, for example, the sacred rock where Demeter sat to rest, and the Well of the Virgins where the maidens, coming from the palace to draw water, found the grieving goddess. Nearby was the dancing field, where the maidens danced in honor of Demeter and where it is believed that temple attendants danced in the sacred rites. In the side of a hill was the Ploutonion, a cave sacred to Hades believed to mark the entrance to the underworld itself.

These relics of Demeter were venerated by the initiates in the Mysteries, who also contributed monies to build an imposing sanctuary at Eleusis. First, a small shrine was built, then a temple and finally the great Telesterion, a Temple to Demeter which housed the Hall of Initiation for the Mysteries. This great assembly hall could hold 3000 worshippers, and deep within its recesses was the Anaktoron, or Adyton, the room that held an ancient wooden statue of Demeter. Here the priests conducted the most secret and sacred of the Mysteries.

The entire sanctuary was protected by walls and entered through monumental gateways. Such was the reverence for the sanctuary, however, that no impious armies ever attempted to seize Eleusis. In fact, there was a truce for all hostilities in Greece at the time of the celebration of the Mysteries, so that the faithful could attend. Twice a year, in the winter and in the fall, the truce was enforced, so that candidates could travel to Eleusis for initiation and then return again for further celebration of the Mysteries. The celebrations culminated in a torchlit procession from Athens to Eleusis; in all the years that the Mysteries were celebrated this procession was only once cancelled, when the celebrants learned that Alexander the Great had just destroyed Thebes.

Only one man is known to have entered the sanctuary and stood in the Anaktoron itself without having been inducted into the Mysteries: the philosopher-emperor Marcus Aurelius. And such was his reverence for the Mysteries that the emperor left the sanctuary richer than he found it, and never spoke of the Mysteries that he had seen at Eleusis.

EPIDAUROS

Whereas Eleusis was open only to initiates in the Mysteries, Epidauros, the vast shrine dedicated to the god of healing Asklepios, was open to all. Although games were held at Epidauros every four years in honor of Apollo's son Asklepios, the sanctuary was thronged with pilgrims all the year round.

Asklepios's origins are unclear; in some legends, he begins life as a hero, and later earned elevation to the rank of a deity. According to some legends, Asklepios came from Thessaly in the north down to the Argolid, where Epidauros is located; in other legends, Asklepios was born in the Argolid itself. Some believed that Asklepios was himself raised by the wise centaur Chiron, who later raised the great hero Achilles. Whatever his origins, Asklepios early became identified with Epidauros, which became his principal sanctuary.

Asklepios offered to his followers one of life's greatest gifts, the gift of good health: when the art of medicine was a mixture of common-sense, herbal lore and occasional desperate sallies with the knife, health

Right: Reconstruction of the great temple at Epidauros, the most frequented shrine of Asklepios, the god of healing.
Bottom right: Remains of a statue from the sanctuary, where thousands of pilgrims sought healing through dreams by sleeping in the temple precincts.
Below: The mysterious *tholos* at Epidauros, built by Polykleitos the Younger for religious purposes now obscure. Its elaborate substructure suggests that it may have housed the serpents sacred to Asklepios.

was highly prized. As we know from attributed notebooks to the famous fifth century BC physician Hippocrates, ancient physicians were baffled by many of the illnesses which they observed. Hippocrates himself evidently thought that many illnesses were caused when food was not digested properly and air or gases formed by the undigested food harmed the body.

The lack of many known treatments or cures led many physicians to conclude that the best healer of disease was Nature. Most Greeks, however, hoped to give nature a helping hand when illness struck, and they turned to a variety of sources of help: physicians, the gods, amulets and incantations, and a practice known as 'incubation,' which was particularly associated with Asklepios. Most Greeks believed that their dreams often revealed the future, or the truth about a vexed issue. Incubation simply sought to conjure up a specific dream with a specific answer at a specific time. The patient slept in the temple precinct and hoped that Asklepios would, in a dream, reveal the best cure.

Of all the sanctuaries of Asklepios, Epidauros was the most important and the one at which incubation was generally believed to have the best chance of success. Therefore, countless pilgrims and their desperate families made their way to the shrine at Epidauros and, after purifying ceremonies, slept in the temple precincts, hoping for a dream that would tell them how best to cope with their illness. In consequence, much of the shrine at Epidauros was taken up by long *stoas*, or halls, in which the patients slept while waiting for both dreams and cures.

Near the *stoas* was the great Temple of Asklepios and the smaller temples of Artemis and Themis, all of which were decorated with thank-offerings left by grateful pilgrims. Some erected lengthy inscriptions detailing the onset, course and cure of their illness. Others dedicated silver and gold anatomical models of the part of the body which had been cured: a silver foot, a golden breast or a replica of a cured infant.

Above: In the fifth century BC, the now desolate shrine at Epidauros was decorated with innumerable thank-offerings from grateful pilgrims who had experienced healing at the sanctuary.
Right: The theater at Epidauros seated 14,000 for the performance of tragedies and lighter dramas in honor of Asklepios and his father, Apollo. It overlooked the fertile Argive Plain, heartland of the Argolid, which many believed to be the birthplace of the god of healing.

The Temple of Asklepios contained a monumental gold-and-ivory statue of Asklepios, similar to that of Zeus at Olympia, or Athena in the Parthenon at Athens. As at Olympia and Athens, the statue of the god was hidden within the temple and visitors were allowed to view it only on rare occasions. Near the Temple of Asklepios was a mysterious round *tholos*, similar to the one at Delphi. Both buildings were evidently used for religious purposes, but their function is no longer understood. The *tholos* at Epidauros was built by the famous Polykleitos the Younger, and some believe that it housed the serpents sacred to Asklepios. Certainly it had a particularly elaborate substructure, suitable for any number of sacred serpents, while the architectural ornamentation (some of it carved by Polykleitos himself) was especially ornate and lavish.

The most impressive monument at Epidauros, however, was the theater, which seated 14,000 spectators in 55 rows. As Pausanias remarked, 'The Epidaurians have a theater in their sanctuary that seems to me particularly worth a visit.' The theater, built deep into a steep hillside, has an upper and a lower section, divided into 12 wedge-shaped portions, and overlooks the rich Argive plain. Like a great semi-circular funnel, the theater looks down on the round orchestra where the performances in honor of Apollo and Asklepios took place.

For the Greeks, performances of the tragedies were but one of a number of ways of honoring the gods. The first performances were dances and songs in honor of local deities, and the great fifth-century tragedies were elaborate enactments of myths staged in honor of the gods. The seriousness of the tragic performances was usually broken by the presentation of lighter plays, the comedies and the Satyr plays.

At Epidauros, the performances in the theater and the dedications in the Temple of Asklepios were all in honor of the god of healing, himself son of Apollo. Apollo partook of his son's honor at Epidauros, but had shrines uniquely his own at Delphi, which housed his sacred oracle, and Delos, believed by many to be his birthplace.

DELOS

Above: Remains of the great torso of Apollo on the island of Delos, an important pan-Hellenic shrine that was also a significant seaport. The powerful Athenians sought to link this island to their city through myth and ritual, although it had been a place of worship for several thousand years before their ascendancy.
Right: Delos boasted beautiful homes with mosaic work to equal that of Pompeii or Ephesus. Despite its small size and barren soil, Delos grew rich as Apollo's sanctuary.

One of the smallest of the Cycladic Islands (only three miles long and one mile wide), the barren island of Delos was one of the most important of the Greek religious sites. The Sacred Precinct and nearby settlement covered almost every inch of the rocky island, which depended on rain for its source of water. Yet despite its isolation and desolation, Delos was a religious site as early as the third millenium BC.

Just as Eleusis owed its importance to the goddess Demeter, Delos was sacred to the god Apollo. As the myths had it, Apollo's mother Leto sought refuge at Delos when she was pregnant and about to give birth. The father was Zeus himself, king of the Olympian gods and, as usual, Zeus's wife Hera was enraged at Zeus's infidelity. Rather than vent her spleen at her husband, Hera pursued the unfortunate Leto, who fled from island to island, grove to grove, mountain to mountain until she finally hid from Hera on the inconspicuous island of Delos.

As it happened, Delos itself was a maiden or nymph named Asteria, who had fled across the Aegean to avoid the passions of Zeus. To hide from the amorous Olympian, Asteria assumed the form of an island, and was thus able to offer sanctuary to Leto, whose plight she could easily understand. Still, Asteria was understandably nervous about what revenge Hera might take on anyone who assisted Leto, and it was only when Leto promised the island-nymph eternal fame that she hid Leto beneath a majestic palm tree, where she soon gave birth to the infant

Apollo and his twin sister Artemis. Thereafter the island was known both as Ortygia ('Quail Island,' from the native fowl) and Delos ('Evident' or 'Manifest,' from the appearance of Apollo).

This was the most common myth about how Apollo came to Delos; in other versions, he came as a youth from Thessaly in the north or Asia Minor. Certainly it seems that Apollo was an important deity for the Greeks of Asia Minor, and as the seafaring Greeks of that region travelled throughout the Aegean they took the worship of Apollo with them. Inevitably, the island which many believed to have been Apollo's birthplace took on a special importance for these traders and sailors. The small harbor of Delos was deepened, and the little sanctuary grew.

Initially, Delos was under the protection of its powerful neighbor, the island of Naxos; as time went by, however, Athens took an interest in the island with its important pan-Hellenic shrine to Apollo. In time, Delos became the headquarters of the Athenian-sponsored Delian

Above: A marble lion from Delos' Avenue of the Lions, a gift to Apollo's shrine from the nearby island of Naxos. These archaic figures (late seventh century) are of Naxian marble, made of one piece with their plinths, as was the colossal statue of Apollo in the sanctuary's center.

League, a loose alliance of sea powers united against the Persian threat with a substantial treasury. In 454 BC, Athens seized the treasury for 'safe keeping,' and removed it to Athens. Not surprisingly, the allies objected, but Athens overruled their objections in the initial steps of the transformation of a league of allies into an empire dominated by Athens.

Just as control of Apollo's shrine at Delphi was hotly contested by the Greeks, so control of Delos was important to the great powers, especially as the island was at once an important seaport and a significant religious site. In consequence, the Athenians tried to buttress their claim to Delos by linking it with Athenian myths, suggesting, for example, that it was at Delos that Theseus had stopped while returning to Athens after slaying the fearsome Cretan Minotaur. Here Theseus performed a mysterious dance, known as the crane dance, which the attendants of Apollo performed at festivals on Delos.

The Delian Festival in honor of Apollo took place every year, drawing crowds from throughout Asia Minor and the islands of the Aegean as well as from the mainland itself. The worshippers streamed along the Sacred Way, which was lined with three great temples of Apollo. Nearby was the Artemision, the shrine sacred to Apollo's sister Artemis, a shrine founded in the Mycenaean era. The birth of Apollo and Artemis was commemorated at the Theke, thought to be the tomb of two of the maidens who had served as midwives to Leto during her labor.

The most impressive monument on Delos, however, was the Avenue of the Lions, a gift of Delos' first protector, the island of Naxos. The lions guarded the sanctuary of Apollo's mother Leto, and were sufficiently fearsome to keep even the jealous Hera at bay!

Like Eleusis and Epidauros, Delos was not merely a religious site but also a civic center, with a monumental council house or Prytaneum and several elegant *stoas* where civic business was conducted. Delos's lovely homes, with their exquisite mosaic floors, rival anything at Pompeii or Ephesus, and speak to the great wealth of Apollo's sanctuary.

Yet, first and foremost, Delos was Apollo's sacred shrine. In commemoration of the god's birth here, no other births (or deaths) were allowed on the little island. All those near childbirth or death were ferried across to the yet smaller islet of Rhenia, which lies just off Delos. So close was Delos' connection with Apollo that a Sacred Lake on the island was the only place in Greece where the god's mantic birds, the swan and the goose, lived. These birds, like the sanctuary itself, were under Apollo's protection, and any harm done to them was harm to the god. Apollo himself, in the form of a 30-foot statue, looked out over the sanctuary which commemorated his birth under the sheltering palm tree, safe from the wrath of Hera.

SOUNION

At the furthermost tip of Attica, jutting out into the Aegean, is Cape Sounion, with its elegant temple to Poseidon. When Athena defeated Poseidon and won dominion over Athens, Poseidon nonetheless was given a shrine on the Akropolis in Athens. When the two deities contested again for dominion over Sounion, Poseidon carried the day and earned the greater temple, Athena having to content herself with a small shrine above the sea. Attica may mean 'the place where the waves break,' and Athenians returning home from voyages to Asia Minor and Delos to Crete and the Cycladic Islands caught their first glimpse of Attica when they saw the pillars of Poseidon's temple shining above the sea at Sounion.

Long before, or so the myths had it, a King of Athens, Aegeus, had waited at Sounion to catch sight of the sails of a ship returning to Athens from Crete. The ship belonged to Aegeus's son Theseus, who had sailed to Crete to fight the Minotaur who dwelt deep within the Labyrinth and each year devoured the maidens and youths which Athens sent in tribute to the greedy beast and the powerful king of Crete.

Theseus had determined to kill the Minotaur, thereby ending Athens' annual tribute. Before he sailed, he had promised his worried father that if he returned triumphant he would change his ship's sails from the black of mourning to the white of victory. Thanks to the Cretan king's daughter Ariadne, Theseus found his way through the labyrinth, slew the Minotaur and fled with Ariadne, whom he promptly abandoned on the island of Naxos.

Ariadne lost no time in calling down the vengeance of the Furies on

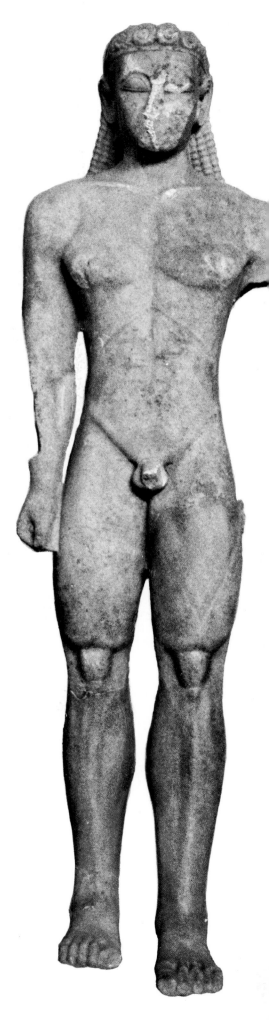

Above: The Temple of Poseidon at Cape Sounion, a landmark for Athenians on Aegean voyages. Here the legendary King Aegeus had awaited the return of his son, Theseus, from the Cretan Labyrinth – and thrown himself into the sea when he believed that Theseus was dead.

Right: Part of the continuous frieze round the inner *cella* of the Temple of Poseidon, attributed to the 'Hephaistion Architect.'

Left: A *kouros* from the original Temple of Poseidon, its face smashed during the Persian invasion of Attica, when statues in the sacred places were thrown down and the countryside was ravaged.

Theseus, with the result that he forgot to change his ship's sails from black to white. In this instance, the sins of the son were visited on the father: when Aegeus saw the black-sailed ship round Cape Sounion, he thought that Theseus was dead and threw himself into the sea. In consequence, the sea became known after the unhappy king as the Aegean. Theseus returned home to rule over Athens and, unlike either Ariadne or his father Aegeus, led a long and happy life, uniting all the peoples of Attica under his moderate rule.

The Temple of Poseidon at Sounion was financed in part with the proceeds of the nearby silver mines at Laurion, which the Athenians controlled and which were one of the principal sources of income for the Athenian Empire. The graceful temple seems to leap skyward above the sea and was always beloved of sailors, whom it behoved to honor the capricious god of the sea. When Poseidon emerged from his palace beneath the sea in his mythical chariot, the waves grew calm.

Right: The temple at Cape Sounion followed the classical Doric pattern, with two columns forming the center of a porch at each end, the whole surrounded by a colonnade of 6×13 columns of local white marble.
Below: Defensive walls on the inland slope of Cape Sounion date from the late years of the Peloponnesian War (fifth century BC).

BASSAE

Countless seafarers saw the Temple of Poseidon at Sounion, but few Greeks ever penetrated into the recesses of Arcadia and saw the majestic temple of Apollo Epikourios which stands in splendid isolation 3704 feet up on the precipitous slopes of Mount Lykaion. As Pausanias mentions, the temple was called 'Apollo the Helper' because the inhabitants of the tiny village of Phigalia believed that the god had turned away a dreadful plague from their people. The temple – designed by Iktinos, the architect of the Parthenon – was their thank-offering to the god whose great shrines at Delphi and Delos already commemorated his healing powers.

Iktinos included in the Temple of Apollo at Bassae a feature that would have been familiar to any who had visited the great temple of Apollo at Delphi: within the temple was an *adyton*, a room that housed the sacred image of Apollo and which was entered only by the priest of the temple. In fact, the *adyton* at Bassae was exactly one-third the size of that at Delphi.

Although the temple at Bassae was of the Doric order, Iktinos included among the column capitals one in the new Corinthian order. The sculptured ornamentation at Bassae (the frieze and the *metopes*) showed scenes from the myths surrounding Apollo and his sister Artemis, and demonstrated their awful power to the worshippers. The temple itself celebrated Apollo's power to ward off the plague, and the sculpture reminded onlookers of Apollo's all-encompassing might: here he was shown slaying the Centaurs, there defeating the Lapiths, elsewhere slaughtering (with his twin sister Artemis) the children of the unfortunate Niobe. When she had enraged Leto by boasting of her many offspring, Apollo and Artemis were sent by their mother to kill them all.

At Bassae, as at all the religious sites of Greece, the message was clear: the gods are all-powerful, all-knowing and, although often placated, may humble mortals and lesser deities with their powers.

Left and above left: Frieze from the Temple of Apollo Epikourios, Bassae.
Below: An unusual Doric base from the Temple of Apollo at Bassae.

6. An Expanding Nation

By the fifth century BC, a truly pan-Hellenic civilization was flourishing. It remained rooted in the mainland, specifically in the *polis* – the city-states that first nourished, then poisoned the Greek ideal – and it shared in the common experiences of such major sanctuaries as Delphi and Olympia, as well as in many secondary locales like Delos and Epidauros. All this is clearly fixed in everyone's consciousness: it remains the heartland of Greek civilization. But there was another Greece also flourishing by this time – the Greek city-states and territories from the western edges of the Mediterranean and eastward to the Black Sea. This spread of Greeks and Greek culture had begun by about 1000 BC, and was generated by a mixture of negative conditions in the 'heartland' – a lack of arable land, for instance, for the growing population – and such positive goals as the chance to prosper by commerce with foreign peoples. And of all the Greek realms abroad, two were especially successful: the Greek cities along the western shores of Anatolia (Asia Minor) and the Greek cities in southern Italy, or Magna Graecia as this region came to be known. And as extraordinary as each of these offshoots of Greece was, each had grown up in a somewhat different fashion.

Previous pages: One of the three Doric temples to Hera at Paestum, Italy, established as a Greek colony 60 miles south of presentday Naples. Paestum's sanctuaries are more intact than any comparable memorial to the Greek world except the Hephaistion in Athens and the 'Concordia' in Sicily.

THE GREEKS IN ASIA

The Greeks who moved across the Aegean to the islands and shore of Asia Minor, whether fleeing the Dorians or not, appear to have gone on their own: that is, there were no city-states to send them forth as colonists (as would be the case with the Greeks in southern Italy). They must have been quite ambitious and enterprising – especially at a time when most of the known world was rather dormant – and they may not even have had to resort to arms when they moved into the choice territories, particularly the best harbors and the fertile valleys at the mouths of rivers. It is possible that these Greeks who appeared in Asia Minor in the years after 1000 BC came more as refugees and immigrants who then established themselves by their industry and wits and were eventually able to impose many of their own ways over less dynamic native peoples.

It is certain, however, that these first Greeks in Asia Minor had to deal with a region and peoples who had long been civilized, who had their own history, culture and traditions. The Hittites, for one, had once dominated much of Anatolia, and they had imposed various social, political, religious and other institutions, but even they were not the first to bring culture to the peoples living along the coast of Asia Minor. These people already had their own temples, for instance, and they tended to worship some variation of the Great Goddess, a sort of 'Mother Nature.' So it was that when these so-called Ionian Greeks began to settle in, they had to deal not only with the native aristocracy or ruling powers but also with the existing religious establishments – temples, priests and deities.

Perhaps the most striking example of this situation was at Ephesus, one of the early Ionian-Greek cities, located near the mouth of the Cayster River (and just across from the island of Samos). Long before the Greeks, long before the Hittites, there had been a settlement and a temple-center where the natives had worshipped a nature goddess. The Ionian Greeks would soon turn Ephesus into the leading seaport of this whole part of Asia Minor and the Greek element – both in terms of population and culture – would prevail. But one thing these Greeks were clever enough to do was to dedicate the major temple at Ephesus

Right: A Hellenistic fountain at Ephesus in presentday Turkey (formerly Anatolia).
Bottom right: The Ionian Greeks of Ephesus built the Temple of Artemis on a site where a similar nature goddess had been worshipped for centuries (550 BC).
Below, left and right: Primitive votive statues from Greek Asia Minor showing the strong influence of Eastern art in this region.

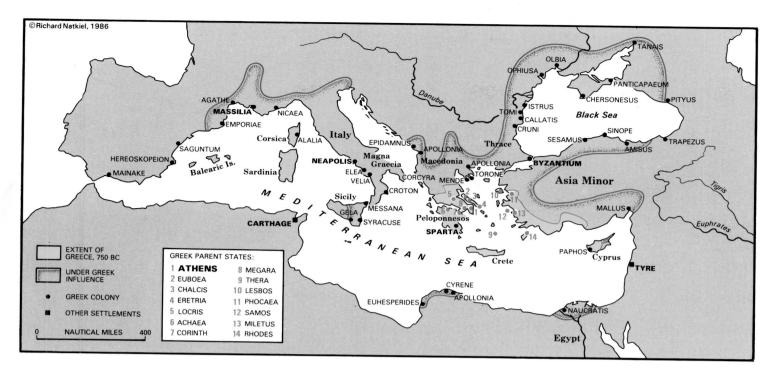

Map labels:

©Richard Natkiel, 1986

TANAIS
OLBIA
OPHIUSA
PANTICAPAEUM
ISTRUS
PITYUS
CHERSONESUS
AGATHE
TOMI
Black Sea
MASSILIA
NICAEA
CALLATIS
EMPORIAE
CRUNI
SESAMUS
SINOPE
Corsica
Italy
ALALIA
AMISUS
SAGUNTUM
EPIDAMNUS
TRAPEZUS
HEREOSKOPEION
APOLLONIA
Thrace
NEAPOLIS
Magna
Macedonia
APOLLONIA
Tigris
MAINAKE
Balearic Is.
Sardinia
ELEA
Graecia
APOLLONIA
BYZANTIUM
VELIA
CORCYRA
TORONE
Asia Minor
Sicily
CROTON
MENDE
5 2 3 10 11
MALLUS
GELA
MESSANA
6 8 4
SYRACUSE
Peloponnesos
1 7 12 13
Crete
CARTHAGE
SPARTA
9
14
M E D I T E R R A N E A N   S E A
PAPHOS
Cyprus
TYRE
CYRENE
EUHESPERIDES
APOLLONIA
NAUCRATIS
Egypt

Legend:

EXTENT OF GREECE, 750 BC

UNDER GREEK INFLUENCE

● GREEK COLONY

■ OTHER SETTLEMENTS

0 — NAUTICAL MILES — 400

GREEK PARENT STATES:
1 **ATHENS**   8 MEGARA
2 EUBOEA   9 THERA
3 CHALCIS   10 LESBOS
4 ERETRIA   11 PHOCAEA
5 LOCRIS   12 SAMOS
6 ACHAEA   13 MILETUS
7 CORINTH   14 RHODES

Above: The Greek World *c* 750 BC.
Left: The Temple of Athena, Paestum.

Below: The Theater at Ephesus, Asia Minor's leading seaport.

Above: Figures from the Nereid Monument or 'Harpy Tomb' (a funeral monument) at Xanthos in Lycia (*c* 500 BC).

Left: A decorative frieze from the funeral monument at Xanthos, executed in the pure Greek-Archaic style.

to the goddess Artemis – twin sister of Apollo (and thus born on Delos with him), probably (judging from her pre-Hellenic name) a pre-Greek goddess, a 'lady of wild things' according to Homer, a virgin goddess, a birth-goddess and a bringer of fertility to humans and animals. Above all, however, she was a goddess who was easily and often identified with a foreign goddess of similar type – namely, the fertility or nature goddess previously worshipped on the site.

And so it was that the Ionian Greeks of Ephesus erected the great Temple of Artemis there about 550 BC, by which time King Croesus of the neighboring Lydians had effectively subjugated Ephesus and many of the other Ionian-Greek cities in Asia Minor. By this time, though, the fame of the goddess of Ephesus was so widespread that even Croesus contributed to the construction of this new temple. The cult of Artemis at Ephesus was also carried by the Ionian Greeks of a nearby city,

Right: The 'Harpy Tomb' took its name from the rapacious winged monster of Greek mythology, who seized the food of her victims and carried off the souls of the dead.

157

Phocaea, and when Phocaeans founded a colony along the Mediterranean coast of what would later be France, a colony named Massilia (later to be known as Marseilles), they also carried the worship of Artemis of Ephesus there. Eventually, the Romans would then take up this cult from Massilia and convert it into their own and similar cult of Diana; the Romans' statues to Diana were therefore modelled after the well-known statue of Artemis of Ephesus.

This is only one of many similar instances of both the intensive and extensive nature of the Greek presence in Asia Minor. Throughout the centuries, too, the Ionian Greeks were constantly interacting with all the other peoples in this part of the world – sometimes as friendly neighbors, sometimes as hostile enemies. The Lydians who, under Croesus, ended up conquering the Ionian Greek cities, had long enjoyed relatively friendly relations with the Greeks; in any case, Croesus himself was defeated in 546 BC by Cyrus the Great of Persia and Lydia and the Ionian-Greek cities were absorbed into the Persian Empire.

South of Lydia and the Ionian-Greek cities was another non-Greek region known as Lycia; unlike Lydia, it never came under any particularly strong political rule, and was eventually absorbed by the Persian Empire. Although Lycia had never attracted the Ionian Greeks to the same extent as the coast to the north, Greeks had still found their way there over the centuries and their influence soon became evident in the architecture and sculpture of Lycia. At Xanthos, for instance, a large tomb or funeral monument was erected around 500 BC; this so-called 'Harpy Tomb' is obviously a work in the pure Greek-Archaic style and other works found in Lycia, both older and younger than this Xanthos tomb, testify to an ongoing Greek tradition. And the exchange did not necessarily operate in just one direction: there was a strong tradition associating Apollo with Lycia, where his most famous shrine was at Patera; Apollo was himself sometimes known as Lyceius, while the name of his mother Leto seems to be derived from the Lycian word for woman, *lada*.

Between the main Ionian-Greek cities on the coast and the region of Lycia was still another non-Greek kingdom, that of Caria. The Carians were said to have settled some of the Aegean islands – possibly even Crete – before the Minoans and then were said to have been forced to retreat to Asia Minor by the Ionian and Dorian Greeks. In any case, they never were able to exert much political power and as the Greek presence in Asia Minor strengthened, the material culture of Caria became increasingly more Greek. Herodotus, the great historian, was from its capital city of Halicarnassus, which at one point formed a league with Knidos, a neighboring city, the island of Kos and the three major cities of Rhodes.

But the highpoint of Caria came under the rule of Mausolus in the fourth century. A Greek-Carian, he was a *satrap* (or governor) of Caria under the Persians, but was left in virtual control of the region. In 357, he supported Rhodes, Kos, Chios and Byzantium in a revolt against Athens, with the result that Rhodes and Kos fell under the rule of Mausolus. He was a curious mixture of Greek and Asian, West and East – patronizing Greek artists and writers but marrying his sister, Artemisia; his fame finally rested on the great tomb of white marble commissioned by his widow at his death about 353 BC. The architect was Pythius, but various Greek or Greek-trained artists worked on the monument for some 50 years; known eventually as the Mausoleum of Halicarnassus and as one of the Seven Wonders of the Ancient World, it had collapsed in an earthquake by AD 1400.

These cities and monuments, then, were only a few of the Greek traces left on the shores of Asia Minor. There were many more Ionian-

Above: This metope at Paestum's seaport, Sele, shows the effects of the city's centuries-long submersion in salt water, following massive subsidence late in the first millenium AD.
Top: Fragments of columns, sculpture and marble dot the sacred precinct at Paestum, at the southern end of the site.

Previous pages: The middle temple at Paestum dates from about 450 BC – contemporary with the Hephaistion.

Right: A section of an ornamental cornice showing the gryphon's head drain outlet.
Below: The strong Doric Temple of Poseidon (actually dedicated to Hera) forms the backdrop for a shaft of 24 flutes at Paestum.

Greek cities – Miletus, Priene, Magnesia and others – and many fine temples and other monuments, all testifying to the strength of the Greek spirit. And as these cities prospered in the Aegean and Eastern Mediterranean world, they also joined such homeland cities as Corinth, Eretria, Athens, Sparta and others in sending colonists and traders to develop still another territory for the Greeks – the shores of the Western Mediterranean, in particular Sicily and southern Italy.

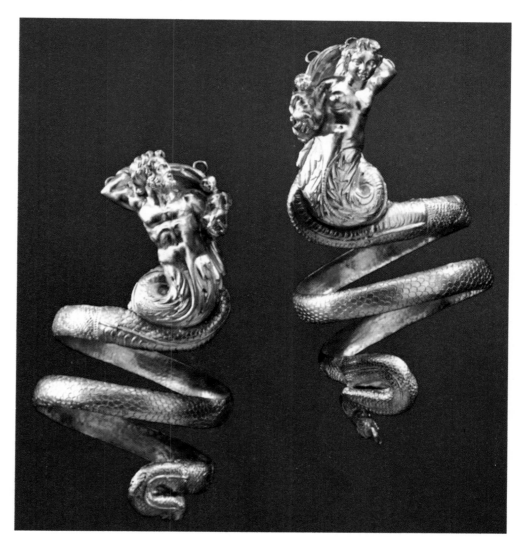

Left: Marble relief of a horseman, *c* 100 BC, believed to be from Rhodes.
Right: Gold armlets representing a Triton and Tritoness, from the third century BC.
Below: The so-called Basilica at Paestum (the earliest temple on the site) shows archaic Doric columns – without bases – that swell and then taper markedly toward the top.

Left: Western Greek colonies like Paestum followed mainland Greece in the simple Doric style. In east Greece and the islands, the Ionic order borrowed its decorative forms from Orientalizing art.

Below left: The Sacred Way at Paestum was one of the first sections to be excavated after this coastal region was drained. To date, only a small part of the ancient city has been uncovered, following its rediscovery by engineers in the employ of Charles III, Bourbon King of the Two Sicilies, in 1752.

This is perhaps the major difference between the Greek settlements in Asia Minor and those in the Western Mediterranean: the latter were founded by Greek city-states that quite rationally and self-consciously sent forth colonists and, at least at the outset, tried to maintain certain links with these colonies. This movement to the Western Mediterranean – as well as to many other territories outside the Aegean 'stadium' – began in the eighth century BC. Merchants and traders had in many instances preceded the actual colonists, but while the former were usually interested in trading Greek or other wares for raw materials, the latter were interested in land they could settle and cultivate. The Greeks colonized many of the choice sites around the Western Mediterranean relatively quickly, and nowhere more so than throughout southern Italy.

By the end of the seventh century, southern Italy was a network of Greek settlements: Tarentum (colonized from Sparta), Metapontum Crotona, Sybaris (colonized from Achaea), Siris (colonized from Colophon), Cumae and Rhegium (colonized from Chalcis); during the next century, Thurii was colonized from Athens and Elea was colonized from Phocaea. Meantime, these colonies were themselves 'spinning off' still more colonies in southern Italy: Tarentum colonized Heraclea, Crotona colonized Caulonia, Cumae colonized Neapolis (later to be known as Naples) and Sybaris colonized Laos and Poseidonia (later to be known as Paestum). By the sixth century BC, these cities and colonies were so prosperous and progressive that they could even support two schools or groups of philosophers – that of Parmenides at Elea and of Pythagoras at Crotona. By about 500 BC, however, due probably to the incessant warfare among themselves and aggravated by the malaria epidemic in southern Italy, Magna Graecia – as their Latin-speaking neighbors called the region – was in decline; only Tarentum and Cumae maintained much independence or distinction after 500 BC, although all of these cities had contributed to transmitting much of Greek culture to the Etruscans and Romans of Italy.

Of all these Greek cities in Magna Graecia, none could claim a more extraordinary architectural complex than Poseidonia with its impressive temples. Poseidonia was a colony of the earlier Greek colony of Sybaris and arose at the end of the seventh century; thanks to its position on the coast it soon became a trading center, and its fertile soil and evidently energetic people must have made it extremely prosperous. (In ancient times it was famed for its pottery and roses.) At a nearby sanctuary of Hera at the mouth of the Sele River, the local Greek inhabitants erected a fine treasury about 560 BC and a temple in about 500 BC.

Not content with these fine structures, the Poseidonians erected three more superb temples between about 535 and 450 BC. The first is known as the Basilica (like all three, it was mis-named in the eighteenth century when the temples were rescued from oblivion) but was actually dedicated to Hera; the second is known as the Temple of Ceres but was dedicated to Minerva and was built about 510 BC; the third is known as the Temple of Neptune, or Poseidon, but was also dedicated to Hera. Standing in what might seem to future generations as a remote and unpromising site, these strong Doric temples attest to the energy and vision of those Greeks who could transplant their civilization throughout the Mediterranean world.

Above: Paestum's *Via Sacra* has been the path to treasures unearthed from the city's ancient civic center; the residential section remains largely underground.

7. Post-Classical Greece

P lutarch, the extraordinary Greek biographer who lived from about AD 46 to 120, recounts a most revealing story about Lysander, the Spartan general who was perhaps most responsible for the victory over Athens in their Peloponnesian War. When the war was over, he found himself involved in a power struggle with the hereditary kings of Sparta and decided that his only hope lay in a change in the constitution that would allow him to be elected ruler; to make such a change, however, he realized he would need the divine sanction of an oracle, and so he turned to the great oracle at Delphi. Now this in itself was nothing unusual: it was in the great tradition of the Hellenic peoples.

But according to Plutarch – who himself became a priest at Delphi – Lysander tried to bribe the Pythia through the offices of some officials at Delphi so that he would get a favorable response. Again, Lysander was probably not the first to have attempted this. But when he failed at Delphi, Lysander did something else: he turned to another oracle, at Dodona, in Epirus in northwestern Greece, in an effort to get a favorable response. When he failed again, Lysander turned to yet a third, the oracle of Ammon at the oasis of Siwa in the Libyan Desert; although centered around the cult of an Egyptian deity, this oracle had long enjoyed contact with Greeks and had even been linked to the oracle at Dodona. Once again, however, Lysander was rebuffed.

Again, many Greeks had undoubtedly tried to influence their oracles over the centuries, but what is revealing here is that Lysander is depicted as simply rushing from one to another simply to get support for his own political aims, even going all the way to the Libyan Desert. Even if the story is an exaggerated attempt by Lysander's enemies to darken his reputation, it is probably expressive of a decline in the prestige of the great oracle at Delphi and the general disintegration of the Hellenic spirit that followed the Peloponnesian War.

Dodona, to be sure, was an oracle of unimpeachable reputation. It was, in fact, regarded as the oldest oracle in Greece, older even than that at Delphi. It was dedicated to Zeus and originally its priests were men; by Plato's time, there were priestesses serving at the oracle. Herodotus says that Zeus 'spoke' in the rustling of the leaves of the sacred oak tree and that his words were transmitted through the beating of a copper vessel with a whip, which the priests then interpreted. Despite its age, the first stone temple was not erected at Dodona until the fourth century

Above: Ephyra, in northwestern Greece, was famous for its Oracle of the Dead.
Bottom left: The elaborate sanctuary featured a complicated passage and rooms of jars filled with sulphur which may have been burned to create a mysterious atmosphere.

Preceding pages: The ruins of Megalopolis ('the great city'), built in Arcadia *c* 370 BC as a protection against Spartan invasion. Excavation has revealed the walls, the great theater and other ruins.

Top: The island of Kos was famed
for the great medical school in the
sanctuary of Asklepios. The most
ancient temple there was built
c 300–275 BC in the Ionic style.
Right: The ruins of the Hypogeum
at Pyli on Kos show the
development of barrel vaulting.

Far left: The refinements of late-fourth-century sculpture are obvious in a bronze recovered from a wreck off Marathon.
Top left: Statue of Asklepios, the god of healing, from Kos.
Left: The Asklepion at Kos is built on a series of terraces with fountains set in the walls.
Above: A fourth-century bronze of the goddess Athena.

BC; a stadium and theater were also erected after this and the sanctuary eventually included several temples. But despite its venerable reputation, the oracle at Dodona never gained the status of that at Delphi – and in support of the interpretation of the Lysander episode, it is believed that Athens never again consulted the oracle at Dodona until the Peloponnesian War. The Hellenic world was definitely beginning to fall apart by the end of the fourth century BC.

As we have seen, there had been competition, rivalry, conflict and even open hostility almost from the beginning of the known history of Greece. But in the centuries following 1000 BC, as the various city-states emerged and as the Greek spirit expressed itself in architecture, ceramics, sculpture and other works, there was a sense that all this energy was at least focussed on some kind of center, some sense of integration: Periclean Athens serves to symbolize this. But quite aside

Below left: The Lion of Chaeronea set up to commemorate and guard the tomb of the Thebans defeated by Philip of Macedon in 338 BC.
Below: The island of Delos, believed by the ancients to be the birthplace of Apollo and Artemis, was sacred to the other Olympians. This is the second-century temple of Poseidon.

from their imperial ambitions, there was something in the Athenians that carried the seeds of their own disintegration. Perhaps it was best expressed by a contemporary Corinthian who said: 'The Athenians are by nature incapable either of living a quiet life themselves or of allowing anyone else to do so.'

The war that broke out between Athens and Sparta in 431 BC was perhaps inevitable and attributable to both parties, but the fact is that Athens seemed to be inviting a showdown. With some pauses, the war dragged on till 421 BC, when a treaty was signed; then, in 415 BC, Athens launched its ill-fated expedition to Syracuse in Sicily; its failure led to a resumption of hostilities between Athens and Sparta in 414 BC, and these did not end until Athens surrendered to the Spartans in 404 BC. The Spartans demolished the Long Walls between Athens and its port at Piraeus; the Athenians' fleet was reduced to little more than some

Above: Arches over a water cistern in front of the theater at Delos.
Left: Fragments of the statues of an Athenian couple Dioscurides and Cleopatra at their house on Delos, *c* 140 BC.
Below: The temple at Lindos on Rhodes was rebuilt in the fourth century BC.

patrol boats; the league by which Athens held power over so many other Greek cities and islands was dissolved; and the Thirty Tyrants, an oligarchy supported by Sparta, took over the government of Athens.

This was by no means the end of the Greek spirit in arts and letters. Ahead, after all, lay the works of Plato and Aristotle, such great sculptors as Praxiteles and Scopas, and innumerable temples and theaters throughout the Greek world. But the rot had undeniably set in. Sparta tried to replace the Athenians in providing some core and unifying force, but Spartans really had little heart or talent for this role. In 394 BC, several major city-states – including Athens, Corinth and Thebes – allied themselves to fight Sparta, with less powerful city-states such as Argos also daring to take up arms. There was no clear victor, and indeed all the Greek city-states lost out as the Persians reasserted their power and in 387 BC forced Sparta to become virtually the Persians' agent in overseeing the Greek city-states. By 377 BC, Athens tried to reassert its power through organizing the Second Athenian Confederacy, but this came to little.

The next city-state to assert itself was Thebes, which under their great general Epaminondas defeated the Spartans at the battle of Leuctra in 371 BC. Epaminondas now set about replacing Sparta and Athens as the organizing power. He restored Sparta's old rival territory, Messenia, in the southern Peloponnesos, set up the Arcadian League and founded a new city, Megalopolis ('The Great City'), at a strategic point in the Peloponnesos in order to serve as its capital. The city was built between about 371–368 BC, and inhabitants of some 40 nearby villages were forcibly transplanted here. But although a number of ambitious structures were erected at Megalopolis, the city and the Arcadian League did not exercise much power for very long; by 362 BC half the citizens of Megalopolis were fighting on the side of Sparta against Thebes. When Epaminondas died in the battle of Mantinea that year, the short-lived supremacy of Thebes collapsed and the Greek city-states were once again in disarray.

Above: Detailed relief of a ship's stern carved in the rockface of the acropolis at Lindos, *c* 180 BC.
Top right: The theater at the new city of Megalopolis, with the *skena* built across the circular stage floor.
Below right: The front row seats of the theater at Megalopolis were built with heavy stone backs and reserved for the high priests and city leaders.

Above: Marble statue of a young horseman. Second century BC.
Below: The sanctuary at Dodona was rebuilt in the Hellenistic era by King Pyrrhus. The theater is 400 feet in diameter.

Right: The head of the goddess Hygeia, *c* 340 BC, retains many classical features including the serene expression and the stylized hair.

And now they faced yet another threat in addition to their longtime enemy, Persia. Across the northern band of Greece lived a people known as the Macedonians, not completely Greek yet not really 'barbarians,' as the Greeks dismissed most non-Greek-speaking peoples. The Macedonians were hardy peasants, but also included horsemen-warriors among their number; since 413 BC they had been ruled by their own kings. Then in 359 BC Philip II ascended the throne and proved to be a remarkable leader; he reformed the government, transformed the Macedonian armed forces into the most disciplined of the day – with a heavy cavalry, a flexible infantry and a swift navy – and set about expanding the kingdom. As he began to seize territory and cities that belonged to cities of the Greek mainland, the Athenian orator Demosthenes began about 350 BC to make a series of speeches – the *Philippics* – that warned his fellow citizens of the threat from the Macedonians. Eventually Athens and other mainland city-states recognized that Demosthenes was right, but they were never able to stop their own squabbles to organize a true resistance. And so it was that when the Macedonians met a major force of Athenians and Thebans at Chaeronea, in central Greece, in 338 BC, it was the Macedonians who triumphed.

Left: The theater at Dodona in northwestern Greece retains most of its original seating.
Above: The circular stage or *orchestra* of a classical Greek theater is thought to have been copied from the round threshing floor where Bronze Age fertility dances took place.
Right: The ancient city-state of Kamiros on Rhodes commanded the western Aegean sea.

Left: Second-century marble statue of Athena is typical of Hellenistic art, showing strong Near Eastern influences.

Philip II now moved quickly to impose the order that had so long eluded the Greek city-states. He established a new League of Corinth, had himself elected leader, and then allied it with Macedonia in an undisguised effort at ruling all Greece. He then set about a task many Greeks had been seeking to accomplish for almost two centuries: defeat the Persians once and for all. But as he was preparing to lead the expedition of combined Macedonian and Greek forces, he was assassinated in 336 BC. Although his wife Olympias was accused of murdering him, this was unlikely to be true – and in any case, it was her son by Philip who immediately succeeded to the throne. Although he was only 20 years old, he had already commanded the Macedonian cavalry at the victory at Chaeronea, and was an intelligent student of Aristotle. He was, of course, Alexander.

The life and attainments of Alexander the Great read more like a work of fiction than of history, but all that matters in this account is that despite his temporary triumphs, he was unable to establish any kind of lasting and unified Greek state. In some respects he became almost like an Oriental despot, adopting some of the style and ceremony

Above left: One of the later sanctuaries of ancient Greece was at Oropus, where the shrine was dedicated to the legendary king Amphiaraos.

Left: Hellenistic carving including animal feet and elaborate foliage appeared even on the front-row seats of the second-century theater at Oropus.

of Asian potentates and even having himself declared a god. (He had first been 'recognized' as a god, he would claim, by the very oracle of Ammon in Libya to where Lysander had earlier turned.) In other respects, Alexander seemed like a man ahead of his time, particularly in his ideal of the unity of all peoples and his genuine interest in exploration and discovery. His career was too brief and tempestuous to produce any particular works of art in his time, although he left one major legacy to the future of civilization when he founded the city of Alexandria in Egypt. And he certainly introduced Greek art and culture to many remote peoples all the way into India.

But with Alexander's death from fever in 323 BC, his great empire quickly began to come apart. Unable to unite around any heir to the Macedonian throne, three of Alexander's generals divided up the empire among themselves, and by 275 BC, three separate dynasties had been established. The Ptolemies ruled Egypt, Libya, Cyprus and southern Syria; the Seleucids ruled most of Alexander's conquered lands throughout Asia; and the Antigonids ruled Macedonia and some parts of Greece. But most of the Greek mainland cities regained an independence of sorts, even though they were unable to exercise much power. From 275 to 200 BC, most of the Greek world was engaged in one war or another, and only at the end did one of the Antigonids, King Antigonus Doson, succeed in imposing some authority over much of the mainland. But during the 125 or so years since the death of Alexander, a different type of unity was to spread throughout much of his empire – a style of life and culture that has come to be known as Hellenistic.

By eliminating the Persians as a threat and power, Alexander had released many Greek cities in Asia Minor to go their own way again; meanwhile, despite all the fighting among the leaders of the various sections of the former empire, most individuals were allowed to do likewise. The result was a kind of rebirth of the Greek spirit of enterprise and construction: all over the Greek world, temples and sanctuaries were rebuilt or enlarged and old sacred sites revived. On the island of Kos, for instance, the sanctuary of Asklepios enjoyed its heyday during the period when the Ptolemies ruled; here people from all over the Greek world came to 'take the cure' at the hands of the priests and physicians who carried on the traditions of Hippocrates. It was typical, too, of the new spirit of the Hellenistic age that an individual took responsibility for seeking out a cure that, even if it was not 'scientific' by later standards, at least represented a more active human intervention and control.

Delos, too, long one of the major centers of a pan-Hellenic spirit, regained a new vitality after the breakup of Alexander's empire. Delos emerged as the center of a loose confederacy of Aegean islands and began to prosper as never before, both as a commercial and religious center. Because of its strategic location, it served as a major port of call for ships from all over the Eastern Mediterranean and functioned especially as a wheat market. The island was soon populated by traders and others from all over the Mediterranean – not just Greeks and close relatives but also Near Easterners, Egyptians and Italians. Many ambitious structures were erected in this Hellenistic period, beginning with a large theater and culminating in the great hypostyle hall of the Exchange in the second century BC. And just as social, commercial and religious functions overlapped and people from all over the Mediterranean world interacted on Delos, so deities from various religions became intertwined in its sanctuaries. (Once again, Lysander's consultation of the oracle of Ammon had anticipated this development in the post-classical world.)

Another old center of Greek culture that enjoyed a renaissance of

Left: First century BC group of Aphrodite and Pan.
Top: Statue of an old market woman in ultrarealistic style of second century BC.
Above: One of the great works of the Hellenistic period was the Mausoleum at Halicarnassus, considered one of the seven wonders of the ancient world.
Right: Many pieces of Greek sculpture are known only from later Roman copies.

sorts in the Hellenistic period was the island of Rhodes. Steering a clever diplomatic course among the various warring factions, Rhodes managed to advance both its economic and commercial standing. The city of Rhodes gained a prosperity and glamour that made it the equal of other such cosmopolitan cities as Alexandria and Syracuse, while still older Rhodian cities such as Lindos and Kameiros enjoyed another burst of construction.

But it was Rhodes that must bear some responsibility for inviting into the Greek world its final conqueror: Rome. Confronted with a new wave of Macedonian expansionism, Rhodes joined Attalos I, king of Pergamum, in asking the Romans to intervene in 200 BC; by 196 BC, the Romans had indeed put down the Macedonians – but they had also turned their own eyes on the Greek cities and territories. By 148 BC, after a series of interventions that escalated their 'protection,' the Romans simply annexed Macedonia. By 146 BC, and with the destruction of Corinth, all of Greece was effectively reduced to a province of Rome. There was peace, to be sure – the legendary *Pax Romana* – but it was the imposed peace of conquest. And the Romans showed their respect for the great past and culture of the Greeks by building new structures at the old centers of Greek civilization such as Eleusis and Athens.

In that sense, the Greek world never died. Throughout the Roman Empire, in fact, the Greek world – in both its tangible forms and its intangible spirit – was taken up. Sometimes it was adapted slightly, sometimes transmuted greatly. But the true treasures of the ancient Greeks – their accomplishments in the arts and crafts, their attainments in literature and thought – would live on to provide a golden beacon that all could strive to emulate or enjoy.

Left: A Roman copy of a famous statue by Lysippus of an athlete scraping himself with a strigil. The leg brace (a log of wood) was probably added by the copyist.
Below: The Romans conquered the Greek world and Roman buildings joined earlier Greek work. At Argos, Roman baths were built below the Greek theater.

Selected Reading

Alsop, Joseph *From the Silent Earth* (Harper & Row, 1964)

Arias, Paolo Enrico *A History of 1000 Years of Greek Vase Painting* (Abrams, 1963)

Bieber, M *History of the Greek and Roman Theater* (Princeton Univ, 1961)

Biers, William *The Archaeology of Greece* (Cornell Univ, 1980)

Boardman, John *Athenian Black Figure Vases* (Oxford Univ, 1974)
Athenian Red Figure Vases (Thames & Hudson, 1975)
The Greeks Overseas: Their Early Colonies and Trade (Thames & Hudson, 1980)
Pre-Classical: From Crete to Archaic Greece (Penguin, 1981)
Greek Art and Architecture (Abrams, 1967)

Bowder, Diana (ed) *Who Was Who in the Greek World* (Cornell Univ, 1982)

Burn, Andrew *Greek City States: From Their Rise to the Roman Conquest* (McGraw-Hill, 1969)
The Living Past: A Time-Traveller's Tour of Historic and Prehistoric Places (Little Brown, 1980)

Carpenter, Rhys *Architects of the Parthenon* (Penguin, 1970)
Discontinuity in Greek Art (Cambridge Univ, 1976)

Chadwick, John *The Mycenaean World* (Cambridge Univ, 1976)

Cottrell, Leonard *The Bull of Minos* (Grosset & Dunlap, 1962)

Demargne, Pierre *The Birth of Greek Art* (Golden Press, 1969)

Desborough, V *The Greek Dark Age* (Benn, 1972)

Dinsmoor, W B *The Architecture of Ancient Greece* (Argonaut)

Doumas, Christos *Cycladic Art* (British Museum Publ, 1983)

Dunbabin, T J *Western Greeks: The History of Sicily & South Italy from the Foundation of the Greek Colonies to 488 BC* (Oxford Univ, 1948)

Finley, M I *Early Greece: The Bronze & Archaic Ages* (Norton, 1981)

Flaceliere, Robert *Daily Life in Greece at the Time of Pericles* (Macmillan, 1965)

Folsom, Robert S *A Handbook of Greek Pottery: A Guide for Amateurs* (New York Graphic Society, 1968)

Graves, Robert *The Greek Myths* (Penguin, 1957)

Green, Peter *Alexander the Great* (Praeger, 1970)
The Armada from Athens (Hodder & Stoughton, 1970)

Grene, David Lattimore, Richmond, eds: *The Complete Greek Tragedies* (Univ of Chicago, 1960)

Gruen, Erich *The Hellenistic World and the Coming of Rome* (Univ of California, 1984)

Guido, Margaret *Sicily: An Archaeological Guide* (Praeger, 1967)

Hadas, Moses *Ancilla to Classical Reading* (Columbia Univ, 1954)

Hafner, German *The Art of Rome, Etruria & Magna Graecia* (Abrams, 1967)

Hamilton, Edith *Mythology* (various editions)

Hammond, Nicholas *A History of Greece to 322 BC* (Oxford Univ, 1959)
(ed) *Atlas of the Greek and Roman World in Antiquity* (Noyes Press, 1981)

Hanfmann, George *Classical Sculpture* (New York Graphic Society, 1967)

Hawkes, Jacquetta *Dawn of the Gods* (Random House, 1968)

Hogarth, David *Ionia and the East* (Haskell, 1969)

Hood, Sinclair *The Arts in Prehistoric Greece* (Penguin, 1978)
The Minoans (Praeger, 1971)

Hutchinson, R W *Prehistoric Crete* (Penguin, 1962)

Jenkins, Romilly *Dedalica: A Study of Dorian Plastic Art in the 7th Century BC* (McGrath, 1971)

Lawrence, A W *Greek Architecture* (Penguin, 1967)

Lullies, Raymond & Max Hirmer *Greek Sculpture* (Abrams, 1957)

MacKendrick, Paul *The Greek Stones Speak* (Norton, 1981, 2nd ed)

Marinatos, Spyridon & Max Hirmer *Crete and Mycenae* (Abrams, 1960)

Matz, Friedrich *Crete and Early Greece* (Crown, 1962)

Mylonas, George *Ancient Mycenae* (Princeton, 1957)
Eleusis and the Eleusinian Mysteries (Princeton, 1961)

Nilsson, Martin *History of Greek Religion* (Norton, 1964)
The Mycenaean Origin of Greek Mythology (Univ of California, new edition, 1972)

Onions, John *Art & Thought in the Hellenistic Age* (Thames & Hudson, 1979)

Ormerod, H *Piracy in the Ancient World* (Univ of Liverpool, 1924)

Page, Denys *History of the Homeric Epic* (Univ of California, 1959)

Pausanias *Guide to Greece*, trans by Peter Levi (Penguin, 1979)

Richter, Gisela *Sculpture and Sculptors of the Greeks* (Yale Univ, 1970)

Rose, H J *Gods and Heroes of the Greeks* (Meridian, 1958)

Rouse, W H D *Gods, Heroes and Men of Ancient Greece* (Signet, 1957)

Scully, Vincent *The Earth, the Temple, and the Gods* (Praeger, 1969)
The Search for Alexander: An Exhibition (New York Graphic Society, 1980)

Simpson, R Hope *Mycenaean Greece* (Noyes, 1981)

Snodgrass, Anthony *The Dark Age of Greece* (Edinburgh Univ, 1971)

Taylour, Lord William *The Mycenaeans* (Praeger, 1964)

Thomson, George *Aeschylus and Athens* (Grosset & Dunlap, 1969)

Tomlinson, R A *Greek Sanctuaries* (St. Martin's Press, 1976)

Vermeule, Cornelius *The Art of the Greek World* (Museum of Fine Arts, Boston, 1982)

Vermeule, Emily *Greece in the Bronze Age* (Univ of Chicago, 1964)

Webster, T B L *Athenian Culture and Society* (Batsford, 1973)

Willetts, R F *Everyday Life in Ancient Greece* (Putnam's, 1969)

Woodhead, Arthur *The Greeks in the West* (Praeger, 1962)

Wycherley, Richard *How the Greeks Built Cities* (Norton, 1976)

Zervos, Christian *L'art des Cyclades* (Cahiers d'Art, 1957)

Zimmern, Alfred *The Greek Commonwealth: Politics and Economics in Fifth-Century Athens* (Oxford Univ, 1961)

Index

Acknowledgments

The publisher would like to thank
Adrian Hodgkins who designed the
book, Penny Murphy who indexed it
and the following for supplying
illustrations:

Ashmolean Museum: pages 9, 10, 16
  (top right), 127 (top left and
  bottom right), 152–3.
Robert Baldridge: pages 6–7, 15.
Bison Picture Library/Rosenthal:
  page 38 (right).
Boston Museum of Fine Arts/Mansell
  Collection: page 57 (bottom).
British Museum: pages 38 (left), 92
  (right).
Heraklion Museum: pages 18 (all
  three), 20 (bottom left and right),
  22 (all three), 23.
Anthony King: page 187.
Mansell Collection: pages 8 (both),
  12–13, 13, 16 (top left), 21, 36–7,
  37, 40, 41 (all three), 42–3, 43, 44
  (bottom), 45 (middle and bottom),
  53, 56, 92 (left), 104–5, 124–5 (all
  six), 126–7, 127 (top right, middle,
  bottom left), 128–9 (all five), 132,
  141, 148–9 (both), 188.
Metropolitan Museum of Art: pages
  11, 27 (right), 42 (top), 47, 67, 90,
  99 (bottom), 103, 162, 163 (top),
  166–7, 182–3, 186 (top right).
National Archeological Museum,
  Athens: pages 94, 94–5, 95, 121,
  170, 171 (right), 178 (top), 179, 182,
  186 (left).
National Museum, Athens: page 27 (left).
Richard Natkiel: page 155 (top).
Mary R Raho: page 110–11.